The God Who Showed Up

Dr. Peter M. Kurowski

First published by Dog Ear Publishing
4011 Vincennes Rd
Indianapolis, IN 46268
www.dogearpublishing.net

ISBN: 978-1-4575-4802-4

This book is printed on acid-free paper.

Printed in the United States of America

Dedication

To Jim Schutt, whose good questions
teased me into writing this book.

Contents

Duly Noted

Anywhere in this book where Jesus is referred to as the *rising Messiah* refers to a rich metaphor that comes from the excellent book *Jesus: The Messiah in the Hebrew Bible.* Dr. Eugene J. Pentiuc is the author of this first-rate work. Early in his book, he quotes from the Babylonian Talmud, Sanhedrin 98b: *"The world was created for the sake of the Messiah."*

My information on Eusebius and the statistical success of the Christian Church comes from the sparkling work of Dr. Paul L. Maier. His *Eusebius: The Church History* clearly reveals the thesis of *The God Who Showed Up*, as it was a paramount proclamation of the Early Church.

Dr. Paul Maier's nephew, Dr. Walter A. Maier III, spurred me to make reference to Jesus' presence in the Old Testament as the Divine Presence in the Cloud (*Concordia Theological Quarterly*, 79:1–2, January/April 2015, 79–103).

Pastor Jack Cascione has written a remarkable book, *Repetition in the Bible*. This gem reveals the unity of the Bible brought about by the One Author of the Bible, Jesus (1 Timothy 2:5). Also, Jack gets the credit for the theological nugget in the book on Exodus 16:16.

Hebrew scholar Dr. Reed Lessing is the source for Gideon being described as the "Barney Fife of the Old Testament" *until* Gideon met Jesus face-to-face.

Preface

On March 19, 2016, I attended a concert at the historic Finke Theatre in California, Missouri. The presentation was titled "Bach to the Future." Four renowned players enlisted music from Bach, Beethoven, and Mozart to perform magical music in new ways. At the end of the performance, shouts of "Encore!" arose. Standing ovation! Joy filled the air. In sync music, especially within the context of a world that is so dissonant, is delightful!

How glad I was that these four gentlemen *showed up*.

The God Who Showed Up is a book that attempts to do something similar to what these men of music did. It aims at bringing new old sounds to the ears and eyes of people who listen to God with an attentive ear and read the Bible with an alert eye. At the same time, it is a book for those who have tried to read the Bible and have been overwhelmed by its massive history. It is a book to assist readers with a hugely helpful hermeneutical handle. By seeing that they are loved *infinitely* and *intimately* by *The God Who Showed Up*, Scripture opens up to them!

It is a book for milk drinkers *and* meat eaters.

People who have purchased my earlier Bible study on the God who shows up, have on a number of occasions said that it was "electrifying." Others have said, "We have never heard this before." Others added, "We would like to know more."

And so this book, *The God Who Showed Up*, is a sequel to the well-received Bible study *The Angel of Angels*. It aligns with two historical novels I co-authored with Elizabeth Scheperle Raj. These novels, designed especially for teens, tell of how Jesus showed up in the Genesis and Exodus era. He came to reveal how "the hopes and fears of all the years" are met in *The God Who Showed Up*! The "Everlasting Angel" and the "Real Magic" have thrilled young readers who have come to see Jesus' crucial role in the Old Testament.

May this expanded work from *The Angel of Angels* also edify, enlighten, and electrify you as it confesses the good news of Jesus, who is Lord! This book is immensely practical, because peace rules the day when the God who shows up rules the heart. All the madness, selfishness, and lawlessness in the world are the result of people not knowing "the God who showed up." His love, His presence, and His presents alone can satisfy our deepest needs. Above all, receiving this story is the key to an abundant, joyful, and eternal life (John 20:31; 1 John 1:4).

Shalom!

Dr. Peter M. Kurowski

California, Missouri

Good Friday, 2016

1

Visiting Albert Einstein

A colleague of mine once made a cold-turkey evange-
lism call on Albert Einstein. Einstein was at Prince-
ton. My fellow pastor was a Lutheran chaplain there. He
knocked on the door of the famous residence at 112 Mer-
cer Street. Einstein had recently returned home recovering
from gall bladder surgery.

Einstein's receptionist, his sister Maria, asked my colleague, Dr. Nauss, to wait in the vestibule while she went
upstairs to confer with her brother. This was back in the
days before today's less painful, less invasive gall bladder
surgery. In those days, that type of surgery was often a
sicker-than-a-dog weeklong ordeal.

Once a green light was given, upstairs Pastor Nauss
went. There, the future *Time* magazine's "greatest man of
the last century" was relaxing. Sitting in a rocking chair,
Einstein appeared most congenial despite the recent

rugged surgery. Einstein reckoned a theological chat with a Lutheran clergyman just might be...good medicine.

Einstein had a high degree of esteem for the Lutheran pastors in Germany who were Bible-believing and Christ-centered. They were some of the few people to stand up against Hitler. The secular university professors and liberal journalists did not. Invertebrate species of the first rank, the presses and professors looked the other way. Without a moral compass, they lacked compassion as well as courage. Einstein recognized their cowardice while remembering the courage and compassion of Confessional Christians. He grasped the profound *practical* difference that sound theology made.

At one time Einstein looked down upon Christians who took the claims of the Bible seriously. Upon reflection of their profiles of courage, however, Einstein had a change of heart. He saw how decent theology created decent people.

As Pastor Nauss walked into Einstein's study, he recalled the famous bushy silver hair of this genius. That hair stretched out in a half dozen different directions from Einstein's head. Puffing on his pipe, Einstein was relaxed in his rocking chair. His feet were shoeless. His porous socks manifested his toes. All of this made quite an impression upon the young Lutheran pastor.

Early in life, Einstein had, for a time, wanted to be a rabbi. Thus, he was very conversant with the Old Testament Scriptures. But as everyone knows, his passionate pursuit of knowledge would lead him into the vocation of science, physics, and cosmology.

Einstein thoroughly held his own in an energetic, amicable two-hour discussion and debate with the pastor. Dr. Nauss, a capable theologian and a proponent of the "God who shows up," brought before Dr. Einstein all kinds of biblical prophecies.

Einstein was invigorated. He probably had not had a serious conversation with a competent student of the Bible in decades. Most of Europe's theologians, with their crippled Christ-less theology, had paved the way for Hitler, not Messiah Jesus. With an anemic biblical theology, these scholars became "useful idiots," helpful only in bringing about the spiritual vacuum that Hitler promised to fill.

One would have loved to have been a fly on the wall that day in Einstein's upstairs study. Back and forth these two intelligent questers for truth pinged and ponged. Minutes turned into hours.

As the conversation drew to an end, Dr. Nauss asked Dr. Einstein what he specifically thought about Jesus. Einstein responded favorably. He said of Jesus that He was the most luminous person to appear on the stage of history.

Albert Einstein penned for us in other places his thoughts about Jesus. What he said to Dr. Nauss was consistent with what he wrote elsewhere. On one occasion he wrote, "As a child I received instruction in the Bible and the Talmud. I am a Jew, but I am enthralled by the luminous figure of the Nazarene.... No one can read the Gospels without feeling the actual presence of Jesus. His personality pulsates every word. No myth is filled with such life."

Dr. Nauss appreciated the generous response of the great scientist. Still, there was one more probing question that needed to be asked: "Do you believe also that Jesus was the Son of God?"

"No, I do not," replied Einstein.

Dr. Nauss gently but firmly pressed Einstein. "What are you going to say on Judgment Day when God asks you why haven't you received His greatest gift to mankind, His Son, who came into the world for you, died on the cross for you, and rose from the dead for you?"

Einstein did not answer quickly. He paused for a few moments. He puffed from his pipe. He rocked back and forth. By then, after these modest kinetics, a grin emerged upon his mouth. His mind had found an answer he was comfortable in giving to the young Lutheran theologian, chaplain, and pastor.

"I guess...I will...have to tell God...that He did not give me a brain big enough to embrace this revelation."

Actually, Dr. Einstein, in commenting about the *rising Messiah,* quoted the *fallen Messiah.* There, the fallen Adam said to the *rising Messiah* who was walking in the garden, "The woman that You gave me...she is the cause of our eating the forbidden fruit" (see Genesis 3:12).

Oops!

Will Rogers once said that the history of America could be divided into three stages: "the passing of the buffalo, the passing of the American Indian, and the passing of the buck." The "passing of the buck," or *"self-justification,"* is the native path of natural man. To scapegoat things on to God comes all too easy for all of us.

"God, the brain You gave me just wasn't big enough."

In part, Einstein's answer is very understandable. He had grown up in a tradition much like the liberal Christian one. That tradition was beholden to theological legalism. It simply did not emphasize the clear Old Testament theology regarding the Messiah God who showed up with *the gift* of salvation. Thus Einstein did not receive from the Hebrew Bible the cosmic Messiah-centered, grace-centered theology that would have easily had room for his future $E=MC^2$ breakthrough.

Jesus encountered the same deficit in His day. The religious leaders for the most part didn't have a clue about His Messiah-visits *throughout* the Hebrew Bible. Abraham, Moses, and Elijah did, but not the religious leaders. Even though the *rising Messiah's* track record was beyond light-years in scope, the religious leaders whiffed, missing fabulous facets of the Gospel!

Seventy times in the Old Testament, there are *explicit* references to Jesus showing up. He shows up as the God-man Messenger of the LORD. From the first to the last book of the *Hebrew* Bible, His footprints can be seen.

In different centuries and millenniums, the Messenger of the LORD appears in this God-man form (see Genesis 16: 7, 13; Philippians 2:5–6). This does not include the numerous references to the appearances of Christ *in, with, and under* the Divine Cloud and the Pillar of Fire. Here, His paradoxical presence protects Israel in its wilderness years and beyond (see Exodus 14; 23:20, 21, 23a; 33:7–11; 40:34–38; Numbers 12:5, 9–10a; 1 Corinthians 10:5; etc.). His presence here foreshadows His *in, with, and under* presence in His means of grace throughout history.

When this Cosmic Figure appeared, people like Moses and Joshua worshiped Him. They fell to their knees. They realized they were standing on holy ground (see Exodus 3; Joshua 5:13–15). This is powerful prophetic prep work for His more sustained thirty-three-year-long appearing.

And the Word was made flesh and dwelt among us, and we beheld His glory, the glory as of the only begotten of the Father, full of grace and truth (John 1:14).

A historian once observed, "Most people's knowledge of history is like a string of graduated pearls without the string." If one misses the superlative string of God showing up in history during the days of Abraham, Moses, and Elijah, revisionism rules. God's glory gets overlaid with 666 antichrist aid. A different Jesus comes forth other than the Jesus of reality (see 1 Corinthians 11:4).

We will now begin to look at some of these stories in the string of clear Old Testament accounts of the God who enters history. This God of all grace shows up to save sinners, reveal God's infinite love, and restore our broken world. It is the longest-running story in the universe. It is a story that human beings are, from so many angles, incapable of crafting themselves. It is the greatest story ever told. It is a story that has given birth to the deepest displays of love, sacrifice, and nobility in history. Enjoy!

2

The God Who Showed Up

Empty promises litter the landscape of this broken world. People lie all the time. Lies shatter trust. They bruise love. They suck dry hope. They dress up freedom in drag. They are the devil's native language.

Empty promises take many forms. One such form is known as "no-shows." No-shows are Pinocchio people. They promise to be present at an event, but then they skip. They become missing in action—without just cause. With little remorse, they take a different course. Love is not rude, but no-shows are.

Certain music stars are known for no-show performances. Some famous athletes and movie stars also have been known to stiff their fans. Restaurants around the world are robbed daily by no-show customers who junk their word and jettison their reservations.

And so it goes, all these no-shows.

Common to a no-show guy is an affinity for a no-show god. If your object of faith is a god who is a no-show, reliability, fidelity, and integrity will run low.

The object of faith of a no-show person is usually a no-show god. Such a god is opaque and obscure, distant and dispassionate, abstract and artificial. Moreover, this idol is idle. By having a no-show god, humans can twist their vague inert gods into their own self-centered images. No-show gods are the bane of this world, a horror to humility, and a terror to humanity.

Elijah observed this phenomena during the ninth century B.C. He lived at a time when the powers of the demonic ran wild. Ahab, a weak, corrupt king, was a moral monster. He even burned his sons in the fire (see 2 Chronicles 28:3). Jezebel, his wicked wife, was a female Hitler.

Things had come to a head. The God of grace could no longer tolerate the amped-up evil of Dumb and Dumber. A fierce, fiery faceoff was kindling.

The religion of Ahab centered on Baal. Perversion was Baal's means of conversion. Assimilation often included mutilation. *Anything goes* suicidal sex made their baleful god a fatal attraction. Sex trafficking under Queen Jezebel was another feature from hell that marked the malevolent manner of this vile religion.

Jezebel the Bully and her weak husband had lost all sense of right and wrong. They were soulless. Jezebel, through power, money, and lust, had seduced 450 of her pet prophets by profits built on the molested bodies of slaves. Ahab used his power to steal vineyards.

But now judgment day had come. The holy wrath of the God-of-the-Angel-Armies was drawing near. His holy justice and love were ready to launch. To protect the vulnerable demanded intervention. The hammer of God was raised. Elijah was called by the Gospel to take a decisive stand.

The battle lines were clear. Elijah told Ahab to assemble the 450 prophets of the local gods, the Baals, plus the 400 prophets of the whore goddess Asherah. A showdown would occur at Mount Carmel.

Elijah said to Ahab, "Let the Baal prophets bring up two oxen; let them pick one, butcher it, and spread it out on an altar on a pile of firewood. But don't light it. You will pray to your gods and I will pray to the God of Abraham, Isaac, and Jacob. The god who answers with fire will prove to be, in reality, God" (see 1 Kings 18).

Elijah invited the false prophets of Baal to go first. So they slaughtered the oxen and prepared it. And they prayed to Baal. And prayed. And prayed. And prayed. And...there was no answer!

It was now noon. Elijah asked the Baal prophets if their no-show god was asleep. It was clear: Their god was all froth and no beer.

Perhaps, Elijah suggested, their whore goddess was sitting on the toilet? On vacation? With raw, righteous anger, Elijah threw down the gauntlet. His stomach churned, because he saw the predatory nature of these prophets oppressing the vulnerable, destroying lives, enslaving people. This is the ultimate product of no-show gods.

After Elijah's taunts...the Baal prophets doubled their folly.

These 450 pro-porn prophets and drug cartel religionists were going crazy. Jumping up and down around the altar, they groveled, coaxing their nonexistent god to show up. These bloodthirsty fanatics even gashed themselves. These witchcraft-practicing cutters, ever searching for gutters to wallow in the vulgar, disgusting practices of the nations around them, became frenzied fanatics (see 1 Kings 18:27–29; Leviticus 18:22–25).

The object of worship of the Baal prophets was a superstitious, man-made god. This object of faith had a perverse yen for bestiality. Bad roots, bad fruits. Bestiality turns humans into sub-humans. It is amazing that there are even college professors today who advance this hideous contra-civilization behavior.

These regressive progressives of Elijah's day were in step with the finite fallen times, but not the infinite holy eternities. Like every other salvation-by-works religion, the founders who invented these cruel gods crafted them in man's fallen image. Not having a god who was historical, their faith manifested the hysterical.

So, the nonexistent, superstitious queen god of the Baal prophets did not show up.

Now it was Elijah's turn. Would Elijah's God show up? Would faith in the one God who shows up prove to be well-placed? Would the Kingdom of God through King Jesus, only seven thousand strong at that time, reveal a sign of God's presence?

Elijah called upon his God. The God of grace. Holy. Pure. Fair. Not partial. Compassionate. Merciful. Forgiving. Just. Kind. Almighty. Present everywhere. The God who actually shows up on Planet Earth, would He show His hand?

Elijah, whose name means, "My God is Yahweh...the God who shows up...," was confident His God would reveal His power and presence and passion. His track record of keeping His promises: perfect!

Elijah's God was the very same God who broke bread with Abraham, wrestled with Jacob, and walked with Enoch. His God was the very same God who would break bread with the twelve disciples on Maundy Thursday 900 years later. It was the same God whom Moses had met at the burning bush 600 years earlier. It was the same God whom Moses and Elijah both met on the Mount of Transfiguration shortly before Jesus went to the cross.

This God, who came with the salvation-by-grace plan, was also the Eternal I AM. His fingerprints were intimately over all creation. His footprints led to the cross to procure our salvation. His Spirit-filled imprints left the most lavish display of holy love in history.

Studies such as *The Chronicle of Philanthropy* reveal how devout followers of the God who showed up are the single most generous people group in the history of the world. Jesus said of His followers, "You will know them by their fruit." No-show gods *do not* inspire such degrees of generosity. Rather, they inspire in-house murder and outhouse cruelty.

The most reliable people on the face of the earth are devout disciples of the God who showed up on Planet Earth. By no means are these people perfect. In fact, these people, who are prone to showing up, prone to keeping their word, prone to telling the truth, are the first to say, "We have fallen *far short* of the mark" (see Daniel 9:1–19; 1 Timothy 1:15).

To a stale, dark world, followers of the God who shows up keep this world from tipping into full madness. Fed and led by Jesus' means of grace, they run a royal race. This God still shows up with visible signs and has left us an infallible record of His salvation-by-grace story. It is called the Bible. Having a Pentecost picture of God through the Word, His followers have heard the invitation to *mimic* God (see Ephesians 5:1).

Devout followers of the God who showed up make strenuous efforts to make good on *good* promises. Their word is their bond via their *daily* encounter with the Word made flesh (John 1:1–14). They have been deeply inspired by the wounds of Christ. His living promises wrapped in His perfect love have ongoing power. We show up because God first showed up to us—as the Word made flesh and now through the Word of God (see 2 Timothy 3:15–17).

Mike Stoner, a mathematician, said the odds of this God fulfilling *just* forty of the promises He made to people throughout the BC centuries and millenniums regarding His appearance is 10 to the power of 157. You don't want to bet against those odds leaning on no-show gods who have never stepped foot into history. Yet billions of people around the world follow gods who have never stepped foot into our history. They never stepped foot into history because they do not exist (see 1 Corinthians 8:4).

Written miracles. That is what Pascal called these Gospel prophecies that were fulfilled through Jesus Christ.

Pascal was as smart a mathematician who ever lived. A genius, he knew the whole Bible by heart. He saw these powerful printed prophecies as major miracles.

Showing up is 80 percent of life. That adage is attributed to Woody Allen. So even an agnostic like Allen realizes that *showing up is important.*

Sadly, the importance of showing up is not factored in evaluating truth claims about world religions. With the exception of only one religious worldview, Christianity, the world religions tout no-show gods. Only the God of the Bible gives a clear picture of Himself (see Romans 5:8; John 1:14; 14:8–11).

The God who with humans deigns to dine and turn water into wine, He is history's most luminous Vine. Similarly, He unleashes an unconditional love that moves the story of history toward real hope. It is this love story that is the only narrative that really, really rings true. This message causes people to turn swords into plowshares and spears into pruning hooks (see Micah 4:3). This script alone takes down walls of hate and builds bridges of lasting love.

Apart from the love of Christ, everything else is a soiled bandage trying to cure cancer. If Jesus does not show up on Planet Earth, then Shakespeare is correct: History then is, indeed, *a tale told by an idiot full of sound and fury, signifying nothing.*

This little book will take a look at the God who showed up. This God who showed up is the one God who alone inspired in history equality, dignity for all people, and the taking down of slavery. The story of the God who showed up is a Gospel story, a good news story, a great news story. This story fires into veins the goodwill necessary for good citizens to exercise freedom with responsibility.

It was Robert Oppenheimer who wisely said, "In order to communicate an idea, it is good to wrap up the idea in a person." This is precisely the central storyline of the Bible. From Genesis to Revelation, the Bible consistently, coherently, and congruently teaches that God showed up on Planet Earth to bring salvation, to show us what love looks like and what a loving human being should look like. Without that, we have nothing but dung, death, and darkness (see Philippians 3:8 KJV).

The royal record of the God who shows up is right before our eyes. Because of our attraction to distraction, we easily miss it. Jesus encountered this blindness even among His own disciples, despite His palpable, powerful miracles, flawless words, and magnificent signs and wonders. Warped by the world, they missed the time-warp story throughout the Old Testament of the God who showed up. Shortly before Jesus went to the cross to display the apex of God's love, this conversation arose between Him and one of His disciples. The disciples were still not getting it.

Philip said to Him, "Lord, show us the Father; that's enough for us."

"I've been with all of you so long," Jesus answered him, "and you don't know Me, Philip? If you have seen Me, you have seen the Father. How can you say, *Show us the Father?* Don't you believe I am in the Father and the Father is in Me? What I tell you doesn't come from Me, but the Father, who lives in Me, is doing His works. Believe Me, I am in the Father, and the Father is in Me" (John 14:8–11, Beck).

Only His death on the cross and His bodily resurrection would pull the scales off His disciples' eyes and reveal the extraordinary love able to move people to love deeply, wisely, and eternally.

"Father, forgive them, for they know not what they do" (Luke 23:34) are words recorded by a physician from the lips of the Divine Physician. Without this message from the cross, religions lack insight into the depth of God's love. Moreover, without Good Friday there is no message of victory over death! Without Good Friday and Easter and the God who shows up, humanity runs toward warring madness, suicide bombings, and endless failed utopias.

The extremes of utopia and dystopia can only be avoided through Christ's Sophia. That Sophia is the wisdom of the cross (see 1 Corinthians 1:18–24). This is also the ultimate glory of God (John 17:1).

From the gurney of the cross, the Suffering Servant of Isaiah 53 revealed the God who showed up, the only love that makes people *fully* human.

This book, *The God Who Showed Up*, will examine works of Jesus, not only in New Testament times, but especially in Old Testament days. In the mouths of two sets of collective witnesses, we have this miraculous record—right before our very eyes. These things are written that your joy may be full (see 1 John 1:4).

Now let us examine the joy Jesus brought to Abraham in His visit to this man of faith and the Messianic prophecy about a miracle baby to come.

3

Dining with Divinity

When God showed up to visit Abraham, the father of "Israel to be" jumped for joy. Yahweh coming in the veiled form of a man was God's intimate, ultimate "yes" to humanity. Abraham did not expect a visit in the middle of the wilderness during the oven-like heat of the day (see Genesis 18:1, 10).

Out of nowhere, the God of Abraham's praise shows up. As He does, He brings with Him delightful *details* promising a miracle baby. This is one more step in the salvation story. The LORD had recently appeared to Abraham promising this 100-year-old man that the time for their miracle baby was drawing near (see Genesis 17). Now Sarah would also hear from the lips of LORD the divine details.

"Get the fatted calf! Make the best bread! Prepare curds and milk! Hurry!" These were Abraham's instructions when he saw three men standing not far away from him. Two angels accompanied the third Person, whom Moses revealed in short order was God in the flesh (see 18:13).

These intersections where God meets man were part of an *eternal* plan. Paul outlines it in Ephesians 1:3–14. These twelve verses are all one sentence in the Greek. They are also a coherent, dazzling doxological Trinitarian tribute.

God the Father is the *Author* of salvation. Jesus, God the Son, is the *Agent* of salvation. The Holy Spirit, the third Person of the Godhead, is the *Administrator* of salvation. The salvation work of the Three-in-One God is described in this *long* sentence (see Ephesians 1:3–14).

Was Paul part *German*?

Here in the wilderness of Palestine in 1900 B.C., the *Agent* of salvation, Jesus, was making an appearance. His good-news visit foreshadows the Christmas story. Here, too, angelic beings surround the narrative (Luke 2:13). Something *Wonderful* was about to happen. God's grace-laced agenda to save sinners was advancing (see Isaiah 9:6).

Now flash-forward in time some 1,900 years.

Jesus' presence among the Jewish leaders two millennia later did not engender the joy Abraham manifested when Jesus as LORD showed up to dine with him. While

Abraham threw out the red carpet for God in the flesh, the religious leaders of Judah repeatedly sought to murder Jesus (see Luke 4:28–30; John 10:31–33).

Two amazing visitations were made by God in the flesh, yet there were two drastically different reactions. The 26 AD visitation was missed because the 1900 BC visitation had been dismissed. Abraham received God's coming to earth with huge mirth. The religious leaders in 26 AD did not welcome the Lord of history in such a congenial manner. Jesus' reappearance did not fit into their cramped universe.

They presupposed the finite was not capable of the Infinite.

Consequently, they never took seriously all of the biblical accounts in which God walked with Enoch, dined with Abraham, and wrestled with Jacob. They rejected the face value of these accounts. Their object of faith was neither the Word made flesh nor His Word.

Common to God's visitations in history were meals.

In Genesis 18, Abraham was the host. With joy unspeakable, Abraham hurried and scurried to put together a splendid meal (see Hebrews 13:1). Little did Abraham realize that Jesus was bringing an early Advent present to him.

Joy to the world in the form of a miracle-born baby boy!

Now flash-forward in time again to John chapter 6. Jesus is now the Host. Here He performs another major miracle. Ever aware, Jesus enlists five *barley* loaves and two fish to feed thousands, with twelve baskets left over. These seven pieces of food provided the crumbs and oil for a Messianic banquet in the wilderness.

Twelve hundred years earlier, ironically, Jesus had provided a *barley* bread dream for Gideon. In this dream, a gigantic barley loaf of bread tumbled into an enemy camp, causing cosmic confusion (see Judges 7:13). This was a sign for Gideon to take his 300 soldiers into battle to overcome Goliath-like odds.

Earlier, Jesus as the Messenger of the LORD had *appeared* to Gideon, just as He did with Abraham. In Judges 6:11, Jesus as the Messenger of the LORD came and sat under the oak tree that was in Ophrah. Here He began to disciple the "Barney Fife of the Old Testament," Gideon, transforming him into Rambo.

The *barley* loaf dream that Jesus as the Messenger of the LORD gave to Gideon was added grace upon grace upon grace. This sign was one of a string of Messianic markers given to this unlikely hero-to-be (see Judges 6). Once again, the scholars were murky in their interpretations, ignoring the footprints of Jesus. As Johnny Cash said years ago, "The Bible sure sheds a lot of light on those commentaries."

Mirroring how He showed up as God visiting Gideon, Jesus now, centuries later, takes five *barley* loaves and two fish and provides a mighty Messianic meal in the wilderness *again*.

But even before Jesus performed this New Testament sign, He provided a groundwork miracle. He created for the thousands present a royal carpet of plush green grass in the desert wilderness (see John 6:10). As Lord of the landscape, Jesus as the Good Shepherd leads His people by green pastures (see Psalm 23:2).

After the plush, lush green grass was called into existence, Jesus commences with another major miracle. He takes the two fish and five barley loaves, and gives thanks. Then, with omnipotent authority, the God who shows up multiplies His handful of supplies into a warehouse of food.

He makes so much out of next to nothing (see Genesis 1:1).

And He leaves *twelve* baskets for the *twelve* apostles for the *twelve* tribes for the *twelve*-times-*twelve* number of believers that no man can count (see Revelation 7:9).

Jesus created for the thousands present more than enough food to be fed in all-sufficient style! These Israelites, like Abraham, would dine with Divinity! For the last, least, and lost...Jesus finds them, feeds them, and cares for them on every level. He who fed Israel for forty years as Israel-reduced-to-One would feed the five thousand. As God, Jesus is able to set a table in the wilderness (see Psalm 78:19).

The Messianic miracles Jesus repeatedly performed meant little to the religious leaders. The Old Testament was not their ultimate interpreter to reality, but rather man-made tradition. Like Pharaoh in the Old Testament, the more miracles Jesus performed, the more they doubted. This diverse group of religious skeptics, from reactionary legalists to lawless libertines, had too much faith in them-selves and too little confidence in God's infallible Word (see Psalm 119:97–105).

Had the religious leaders been in step with the Law and the Gospel of the Torah, the first five books of the Bible, they would have been open to the über-time-and-space miracles of the Old Testament. The God of Abra-ham's praise was an omnipotent, omnipresent, omniscient God showing up on Planet Earth. Unfortunately, they were not taught that miraculous biblical Gospel pattern.

Shortly after the feeding of the five thousand, Jesus invited the religious leaders to revisit God's Word (John 8:32). If they took God's Word at face value, their faith would have godly value. They would be in step with Abra-ham. The joy of the LORD would be their strength (see Nehemiah 8:10).

Instead they were joyless, jaded, and jaundiced regarding Jesus' appearances to Abraham, Isaac, and Jacob.

In 1900 BC, Abraham welcomed Jesus. He welcomed Him with first-rate hospitality. The leaders 1,900 years later? They greeted Jesus with first-rate hostility.

Rude, impolite, and gruff, they boasted, "Our father is Abraham!" Implication? They thought, they were, saved by flesh not faith, by race not grace.

Jesus told them that if they would continue in God's Word, then they would know the truth and the truth would free them (see John 8:32). For them, man-made security trumped God's universal grace. Many of the religious leaders thought that Gentiles were made to be fuel for the fire of hell. Fortunately, there was the blessed remnant of Pharisees, such as Nicodemus and Joseph of Arimathea, who were open to the Word.

The faith of the condemning Caiaphas crowd was not the faith of Abraham, Elijah, Elisha, Isaiah, Daniel, the prophets and apostles proclaimed (see Genesis 17:5–6; Daniel 7:13–14; Matthew 27:64–65; Galatians 3:26–29; John 3:16). They had no room for salvation by grace, God's universal grace, and little room for God's means of grace.

When Jesus made reference to God's universal grace at work through the prophets, noting this in His very *first* sermon, as well as before the Sanhedrin, the religious leaders went through the roof. They wanted to drive Him to His death over a pinnacle-like cliff early on, and later on—crucify Him (see Luke 4:14–30; Matthew 27:64ff).

Backpedal to John 8, to the prior debate. Instead of staying with the issue, the religious leaders go for tissue. Ridicule. An ancient modern technique. They even called the LORD who appeared to Abraham, Isaac, and Jacob, and now to them, a bastard! (see John 8:41).

Foolishly, they tried to pit Jesus against Abraham. But Jesus had a supreme advantage. Jesus Himself, 1,900 years earlier, had dined with Abraham. *Jesu, Joy of Man's Desiring* was Abraham's creed.

In Genesis, a clear account of how God in the flesh ate with Abraham, walked with Abraham, and promised to bring about a miracle birth for Abraham and Sarah, was written down by Moses. This miracle child the LORD had personally promised to Abraham was to foreshadow the miracle birth of Jesus, as well as advance the salvation story (see Genesis 18:1–15). A year later, this same LORD visited Sarah just as He had promised (see Genesis 21:1).

With similar plain words, 1,900 years later Jesus told religious leaders, "Your father Abraham rejoiced to see My day, and he saw it and was glad!" (see Genesis 17:17; John 8:56). In Genesis we learn that Abraham and Sarah were so happy when the LORD told them this, and they named their child "Laughter," or "Isaac"!

Genesis 18 speaks of how the Lord "appeared" to Abraham by the oaks of Mamre. While Abraham was sitting at the tent door one day, God showed up. The Hebrew language reveals that this is "Yahweh" who appeared, and so the rendering of "LORD." To be sure, this was Yahweh in veiled form, because no human can behold God in His raw glory (see Exodus 33:19–23). Nevertheless, it *was* the LORD!

In Genesis, the God who shows up promises, *"I will surely return to you at this time next year; and behold, Sarah, your wife will have a son"* (Genesis 18:10).

The Person speaking here is Yahweh, the God who *appears*. More specifically, it is Jesus, the Person of the Godhead who consistently *appears* from Genesis to Revelation. He is the Member of the Holy Trinity who appears!

The LORD who caused Sarah to conceive a miracle child and Samson's mother to conceive a miracle child, does the impossible (see Judges 13; Matthew 19:24; Luke 1:37; Genesis 17:1). Common to both of these stories, Jesus as the Messenger of the LORD appeared.

The same thing happens in the book of Judges. Samson's parents were so overwhelmed when the LORD Jesus showed up as the Messenger of the LORD, they thought they were going to die since they were in the presence of God in the flesh (see Judges 13:21). Fortunately, it was the LORD in veiled form, in grace, in love, in mercy, in kindness.

Jesus Himself, Yahweh in human form, shows up to dine with Abraham in 1900 BC. Jesus saw firsthand the great joy on Abraham's face when He presented to him the pre-Christmas gift of a miracle child. As Jesus did so, He was making good on the very first salvation promise given to Adam and Eve in the Garden of Eden (see Genesis 3:15). In fact, the word *Eden* is part of the gift the *rising Messiah* now gives to Sarah. Wonderfully, the words *pleasure* and *happiness* in Genesis 18:12 is pronounced "Eden" in the Hebrew language.

One would come who would crush the head of the devil. His heel would literally be bruised, as spikes were driven into His feet against the hard wood of a tree. This would happen on a Passover Friday. This day was planned before the foundation of the world.

Jesus was already coming in 1900 BC to Abraham, a continuation of His early pre-Emmaus walk in the post-Fall Garden of Eden. He was coming in kindness even then to lead Adam and Eve to repentance (see Romans 2:4). He was also coming in 26 AD when He spoke to the religious leaders of His day. He comes even today through His means of grace and His lifelines of love to feed His Bride, the Church (see Acts 2:42).

The religious leaders of Jesus' day interpreted the Bible minus the faith Abraham demonstrated in Jesus in his day. They floundered badly over time-and-space considerations.

With a finite view of God, they stubbed their theological toes as to how Jesus, who was not yet fifty years old, had been able to see Abraham and Abraham Him. They lacked the joy Jesus brings, the hope His promises inspire, the imagination that faith in Jesus creates, and the love He bestows.

Jesus told them, "Truly, truly, I say to you, before Abraham was born, *I am*" (John 8:58).

So angry did these men become, that they picked up stones to murder Abraham's LORD.

Little did they realize that they were fulfilling the words of the psalmist: *"The Stone which the builders refused is become the Head Stone of the corner. This is the Lord's doing; it is marvelous in our eyes"* (Psalm 118:22–23).

Little did they grasp that standing before them was the One who had made the sun stand still over the valley of Aijalon, the One go-between between God and man (see Joshua 10:13; 5:13–15; 1 Timothy 2:5).

Little do people today grasp that by Messiah Jesus, all things were created and by Jesus all things cohere (Colossians 1:15–17).

4

Both Testaments: Amazing Grace!

God showing up in the Old Testament was not a onetime appearance. If the story of Yahweh in the form of a Man dining with Abraham was the only account of God showing up, one might be extra-cautious about advancing the theme of the God who appears. But this kind of coming in history by God in the flesh takes place repeatedly.

It is not a sporadic, onetime epiphany calling for prophetic reserve. It is not an abstract onetime flash-in-the-pan theophany to write off as a marginal point. It is not a mathematical point, but part of an infinite line.

It is central, continuous, cohesive, comprehensive, and Christ-centered.

The whole movement of the Bible ripples with the good news of how the Word becomes flesh. It is the overarching theme. Both testaments teach it. Any other treatment of sin, death, and alienation, except the salvation work of the God who shows up, is superficial.

Because the matter of sin against a holy God is so grave, God's solution must literally overcome the grave. It cannot be abstract. It will require a *personal* Visitation. Throughout the Old Testament, God's people prayed for such a Visitation (see Isaiah 64:1; 1 Peter 2:12). Ample precedent was there (see Genesis 16, 18, 22, 32).

The Old Testament faithful longed for God to come down for an extended stay and a dramatic display. "Please inspect this broken planet!"—"*I wish You would tear the heavens apart and come down!*" (Isaiah 64:1, Beck).

Dramatically, Jesus did just this. He did this in His thirty-three-year-long Visitation. On Good Friday, He answered the plea found in Isaiah 64:1 definitively with history's most important curtain call. With a bleeding skull on a skull-shaped hill, as the Bread of life, Jesus bled for all the *skulls* of the world (see Exodus 16:16). The Hebrew word *Golgotha* is literally and prophetically given in the text of Exodus 16:16: "give to each of the *skulls* 48 ounces of bread."

On the cross anchored in that skull-shaped hill, Jesus willed Himself to die. A miracle. This took place precisely at the moment when the Passover Lamb was slain (see Matthew 27:46–50). Another miracle. At that moment the

THE GOD WHO SHOWED UP

thick temple curtain was torn in two, from top to bottom. A third miracle. At the same time, bodies of Old Testament believers came out of the ground. Another miracle! Then a Roman centurion, who was the only one to get right the mission of Jesus in the Gospel of Mark prior to the resurrection, declared, "This Man certainly was the Son of God!" (Mark 15:39). One more miracle.

Regarding the famous temple curtain consider this. The dividing curtain had embroidered on it the *constellations* of the *heavens* (see Matthew 27:51). The ancient pious prayer that the heavens would be split open and God would come down was answered that moment (see Isaiah 64:1). Another miracle. This was conjoined with the stirring resurrection valley of dry bones, the miracle of bodies of Old Testament believers coming out of the ground (see Ezekiel 37; Matthew 27:51–52).

Hand in glove, the two testaments rooted in love reveal the God from above who came down and split open the heavens! In Jesus' baptism the heavens were torn open (see Mark 1:10), and on Good Friday the constellations on the curtain were torn open, along with the graves that were split open (Matthew 27:51). The same root Greek word is present in all three *schisms*.

God showing up repeatedly in the Old Testament, along with His substantial thirty-three-year sojourn in the New Testament, speaks volumes about the unity of the two testaments. Same message. Salvation by grace. Same message. Righteousness is a gift. Same message. God so loved the world that He continually breaks into history in the person of Jesus.

Jesus put forth this message succinctly: "For God so loved the world, that he gave His only begotten Son, that whosoever believeth in Him should not perish, but have everlasting life" (John 3:16). This was the same message when God sent Jonah to the Ninevites. However, the fish-bound prophet was against it. Foolishly, he tried to run away from a God who is everywhere. He tried to run away from the LORD (see Jonah 1:3).

The pouting prophet was furious about this unconditional love of Yahweh, the God of grace. After 100,000-plus Ninevites received the *gift* of repentance (see Acts 11:18), Jonah was fit to be tied. Angrily he said to God, "I just knew you were going to do something like this for you are a gracious God, and merciful, slow to anger, and of great kindness" (Jonah 4:2). Then he stomped off.

The foundational creed in the Old Testament is a Gospel theme. In Exodus 34:6, we see a powerful "Amen" to the grace of God the Father and God the Son as central to Israel's faith: *"The LORD, the LORD, merciful and gracious, longsuffering, and abundant in goodness and truth."* It comes shortly after Jesus as the Angel of God had saved the children of Israel by water and the Word (see Exodus 14:13;

19). In fact, the very root *salvation* word for *Jesus* is nestled in verse 13; it is often translated *"salvation"* or *"deliverance."*

The message of the God who shows up appears not only in Genesis 18, where God visits Abraham, but also in John 3:13, where God visits Nicodemus. The object of faith for Abraham was Jesus. The object of faith for Nicodemus became Christ. And this was the same object of faith for all Old Testament believers (see Hebrews 11; Hebrews 12:1–3; Acts 16:31).

Behold how this is richly rooted and revealed early in Genesis! Examine Genesis 5. See the object of faith of the pre-Flood patriarchs. This good news Messianic message of God coming down to visit Planet Earth should have been part of the Gospel storyline in the movie *Noah* starring Russell Crowe. But the hollow wood of Hollywood built a leaky ark. This badly mistaken movie was devoid of the wood of the cross. It could not handle the scandal of salvation.

What a twisted movie the 2014 *Noah* was. It ignored key pieces of biblical revelation. It falsified the character of Noah. About the only thing the agnostic producers got right in that movie was that they did not land the ark on Gilligan's Island!

The reality? There is *amazing grace* found in Genesis 5. There are *ten* patriarchs listed in this pre-Flood chapter. The Holy Spirit throughout the whole Bible loves using numbers like 10, 7, and 12 in a miraculous, meticulous meter manner.

The book *Repetition in the Bible* by Lutheran pastor Jack Cascione skillfully brings this out. It is one of the best contemporary books written for the serious Bible student. But be prepared to roll up your sleeves for action as you fix your hope completely on the grace that has been brought to you through the revelation of Jesus Christ (see 1 Peter 1:13).

Take a look at the billboard-like Gospel message nestled in Genesis 5. Gospel alive! See Jesus Christ! Now splice! Watch the meaning of the words of the ten patriarchal names tell the Gospel story. Behold the Messianic magic!

Adam means "man."

Seth means "appointed."

Enosh means "mortal."

Kenan means "sorrow."

Mahalael means "the blessed God."

Jared means "shall come down."

Enoch means "teaching."

Methuselah means "His death shall bring."

Lamech means "the despairing."

Noah means "comfort or rest."

Splice together the meaning of these names. What do you get? This Messiah-centered message: *Man was appointed to be mortal. This was very sorrowful, indeed. However, the blessed God promised to come down, teaching how His death shall bring the despairing comfort and rest* (see Romans 6:23; Isaiah 40–53, Matthew, Mark, Luke, and John).

See the theology of the cross present already early in Genesis? Christmas, too? Also Easter? It is hinted at in Genesis 3:15, amplified in Genesis 5, and magnified in Genesis 22:12–18.

Looking back from God's greatest demonstration of His glory, Good Friday, we see the cosmic connections via the Moriah Messiah who shows up to save Abraham's only son. Genesis 22 provides a clear picture of the passion of the LORD. It is a towering type of how God's only begotten Son, Jesus, would provide the ultimate sacrifice on the ultimate altar of the cross (see Genesis 22:12–18).

What a weave! No set of editors could create, cobble, and craft such a story. This story has had lasting power for millennia. It is also the most lofty love story of all history. It has inspired, as C.S. Lewis noted, the greatest love poetry, some of history's greatest literary works, like *Crime and Punishment* and *The Chronicles of Narnia*, and the widest, deepest, and highest charity (see 1 Corinthians 13). It has turned terrorists into apostles of love! (see Acts 9).

Years ago I read Isaiah 53 to a Jewish lady. Isaiah has been called the fifth evangelist. In Isaiah's song on the Suffering Servant, Israel reduced to One, we see a picture of Jesus, the Messiah. It gives a graphic picture of Jesus hanging on the cross, atoning for the sin of the world. This vision is presented 600 years in advance. Here is Isaiah's powerful Good Friday prophecy:

Surely He has taken on Himself our suffering and carried our sorrows, but we observed that God had stricken, smitten, and afflicted Him. And certainly He was pierced for our transgressions and crushed for our sins; by His punishment, we were saved and by His wounds we were healed. We have all gone astray like sheep. Everyone of us has turned to go his own way, and the LORD has punished Him for the sins of us all. He was oppressed and mistreated without opening His mouth. Like a lamb He was led away to be slaughtered. Like a mother sheep is silent before the men who cut her wool, so He doesn't open His mouth. After He was tried as a prisoner, He was then taken away. Who is His time even considered that He was cut off from the land of the living and struck down for His people's sins? They assigned Him a grave with criminals and with a rich man in His death though He hadn't done any crime or said anything deceitful (Isaiah 53:4–9).

After I read this passage to the Jewish lady, she became quite perturbed. She told me, "Stop reading the New Testament to me." I told her, "Ma'am, this is from your own

Hebrew Bible." She turned her head, refusing to look at the Old Testament words.

Nevertheless, this lady understood that Isaiah was referring to Good Friday. Isaiah was pointing to the death of Jesus as the Yom Kippur sacrifice for the sins of the world. The lady saw clearly the theology of the cross in the Old Testament. She *listened* to the text, but she did not *hear* it.

The Old Testament provides the foundation. The New Testament provides the Temple—the God who shows up. Unlike *any other* religion, the Old Testament provides powerful written pinpoint prophecies.

The Old Testament tells how the Messiah would be born of a virgin, be born in Bethlehem, live in Nazareth, be betrayed for thirty pieces of silver, die for the sins of the world, rise from the dead, die between two thieves, be buried in a rich man's tomb, and so much more! Without the New Testament fulfillment, these Old Testament prophecies become a dead stump. With the New Testament fulfillment, we have mighty written miracles.

The fact that the message of these two testaments taken together take down slavery, advance human equality, and spur on the greatest philanthropy, is meaningful to anyone interested in truth and kindness. Former agnostic Rodney Stark in his book *For the Glory of God* demonstrates how God's Word was able to stimulate the rise of science while

Islam could not (p. 2). The quintessential Newton, as well as the more mature Einstein, realized the power that came from the mouth of these two witnesses, these two testaments, the prophetic Old Testament and the apostolic New Testament. Both Newton and Einstein left this world thoroughly pessimistic about *human* solutions to the deepest ills of humanity.

Saint Augustine, the Einstein of the fourth century, also was pessimistic about worldly solutions to the evils of man. He tried almost every ideology and religion possible in his day and saw them as useless at the end of the day. Only when Augustine discovered by grace a revelation that came to him from outside himself did hope spring eternal. Then he realized the tandem revelatory power of the two towering testaments. This great theologian from North Africa saw how these two testaments were in *completely* in sync. Augustine described the wonderful Gospel unity of these two testaments which are really one at the end of the day, this way:

The New is in the Old contained.

The Old is in the New explained.

The New is in the Old latent.

The Old is in the New patent.

Both testaments confess the same God, *very God of very God, Immanuel,* the God who showed up. Amazing grace from the God who comes into time and space to take our place enduring disgrace so that we might see the face of God. These powerful appearances by the God who shows up, not bound by time and space, move millions to confess at the table of the Lord:

Here, O my Lord, I see Thee face to face;

Here would I touch and handle things unseen;

Here grasp with firmer hand the eternal grace,

And all my weariness upon Thee lean.

—"Here, O My Lord, I See Thee Face to Face," v. 1

5

The Full Red-Letter Edition of the Bible

Have you ever owned a red-letter edition of the Bible? These Bibles print in red letters the recorded words of Jesus in the New Testament. With reverence for the Bible in general and for Christ's words in particular, the red-letter edition is commendable.

Still, I am ambivalent about red-letter Bibles. On the one hand, I esteem highly the very words of Christ that have been faithfully handed down to us via the sacred Scriptures. On the other hand, the words of Jesus are not only in the New Testament but also in the Old Testament. The following words, for example, should also be set in red letters: *"I'll come back about this time next year, and when I do, Sarah will already have a son"* (Genesis 18:10). They, too, are the actual words of Jesus.

By failing to put in red letters Jesus' words from the Old Testament, the red-letter-edition editors suggest to the unaware that Jesus did not show up and speak to people in Old Testament times. Yet Jesus did show up and He spoke as we just noted also in the Old Testament era. His words and deeds are quoted by Moses and the prophets (see Luke 24:27). Joyfully, we celebrate all of Jesus' words.

In one sense *all* the words of the Bible should be set in red letters. Jesus as the one Mediator between God and man inspires and mediates *all* of the Scriptures (see 1 Timothy 2:5). In the end, He who died for us, also suffered on the cross, went to hell for us, rose for us, and bequeaths to us the infallible Word of God from Genesis to Revelation.

Allow me to cite the chief means of how God shows up in the Old Testament, how He helps the down and out and speaks clear red-letter-edition words. He does this as the Messenger of the LORD. This Messenger, sometimes also translated as the Angel of the LORD, spoke with the voice of God to Moses face-to-face (see Deuteronomy 34:10).

The first explicit "Messenger of the LORD" or the "Angel of the LORD" account comes from Genesis 16:6–16. In the Hebrew, this title transliterated is pronounced *"Malek Yahweh."* *Malek* is the sound of the Hebrew word for "angel" or "messenger." The Hebrew for *"LORD"* is "Yahweh."

This Angel throughout the centuries has been recognized by Christians as Jesus. It is Jesus making a series of preincarnation visits to Planet Earth as an *uncreated* Angel (*Angelus increatus*).

Eusebius of Caesarea (c. AD 260–339) is considered the father of Church history. A man of massive erudition, he tells the story of the rise of Christ and Christianity during the first three centuries. Eusebius gives insight into the thinking of the early Church.

In ten volumes of his *Church History*, we have a goldmine of data revealing what the early Church believed. He shows how the early Church believed the Christ of God appeared to Abraham, taught Isaac, spoke to Jacob, and conversed with Moses and the later prophets. In his *Church History*, Eusebius wrote these words about the preexistent Christ. Paul L. Maier translates in a lively, faithful fashion the towering testimony of Eusebius about the **nature of Christ**:

His character is twofold: like the head of the body in that he is regarded as God and yet comparable to the feet in that he put on humanity for the sake of our salvation, a man of passions like ours. If I begin his story with the principal and most basic points to consider, both the antiquity and divine character of Christianity will be demonstrated to those who suppose that it is recent and foreign, appearing only yesterday.

No language could adequately describe the origin, essence, and nature of Christ, as indeed the Holy Spirit says in prophecy: "Who shall declare his generation?" [Isa. 53:8]. For no one knows the Father except the Son, and no one has fully known the Son except the Father who begot him. And who but the Father could conceive the Light that existed before the world, the Wisdom that preceded time, the living Word that was in the beginning with the Father and was God? Before all creation and fashioning, visible or invisible, he was the first and only offspring of God, the commander-in-chief of the spiritual host of heaven, the messenger of mighty counsel, the agent of the ineffable plan of the Father, the creator—with the Father—of all things, the second cause of the universe after the Father, the true and only begotten Child of God, the Lord and God and King of everything created, who has received lordship, power, honor, and deity itself from the Father. According to the mystic ascription and divinity to him in the Scriptures:

In the beginning was the Word, and the Word was with God, and The Word was God.... All things were made by him, and apart from him nothing was made [John 1:1, 3].

Indeed, this is also the teaching of the great Moses, the earliest of all the prophets, when by the Holy Spirit he described the origin and ordering of the universe: The Creator gave over to none but Christ himself the making of subordinate things and discussed with him the creation of man: "For God said, 'Let us make man in our image and likeness'" [Gen. 1:26]. (End of Maier's quote)

Indeed, Moses records for us in Genesis the first explicit appearance of the Messenger of the LORD. The setting is eleven years after the LORD by His mighty promises called Abraham and Sarah out of Mesopotamia. To Abraham and Sarah were given gargantuan grace-grounded promises by which all the families on earth would be blessed (see Genesis 12:1–3).

Looking back, we see today the fruit of these powerful promises. Biblical scholar Paul Maier notes how the Kingdom of Messiah Jesus "is the most successful single phenomenon, statistically considered, in all of history." At first, the family of Abraham, Isaac, and Jacob, also the family of our Lord Jesus, struggled. It was fragile, often hanging by a thread. The devil did everything he could to snuff it out. Looking back, we see the Kingdom promises fulfilled in fantastic fashion.

In time, more details were given to Abraham and Sarah. First milk of the Word, then meat of the Word. All along, God was stretching their faith, and, consequently, their love for Him and for others. God assured them they would have a miracle child.

As time dragged on, Abraham and Sarah felt they had to help out an *almighty* God. Like most biblical scholars of today, they presupposed that God could not provide the miracle His promises presupposed. This was an ancient malady.

God told Abraham and Sarah they would have their very own son from Sarah's womb (see Genesis 15:1–6). From their finite point of view, the biological clock for Sarah was already past midnight. The good news was that in the beginning, they received God's promise and believed God's promise and it was reckoned unto them as righteousness (see Genesis 15:6). The bad news is that the virus of salvation by works had slipped into their hearts.

Now, watch what happened. Abraham and Sarah came up with a birdbrain idea. Their plan to help God involved junking the nuclear family. This was a gift Jesus gave to mankind in the beginning with Adam and Eve and that He reaffirmed in person in Matthew 19.

The woebegone couple tried a form of polygamy. Sarah suggested to her gullible husband that he should eat of the sexual fruit of another tree, namely, that of Hagar, her maid. Her plan to provide a proxy mom turned into a bomb.

Big bad idea.

Well, this union ignited an in-house war. Abraham had sex with Sarah's Egyptian maid, Hagar. A boy was born who would be given the name of Ishmael. This departure from the nuclear family contributed to Ishmael becoming an assertive, wild, and surly man. With the birth of Ishmael, Sarah became jealous. No unconditional love here.

She treated Hagar horribly. She learned the folly of departing from Jesus' original plan.

Sarah's salvation-by-human-works plan came to a boil after Ishmael's birth. Sarah told Abraham, "It's all your fault that I am suffering this abuse. I put my maid in bed with you and the minute she knows she's pregnant, she treats me like I'm nothing. May God decide which of us is right" (Genesis 16:5, *The Message*).

Bold and beautiful Sarah became bold and brutal Sarah. She became so abusive to Hagar that Hagar took off running. Distraught, with no social safety nets in those days, Hagar found herself in the wilderness, on the road to Shur, but unsure where she was going to go.

Down and out, very vulnerable in that lawless age, she would have been easy pickings for slavery and her son was ripe for pagan child sacrifice. Blessedly, the God who shows up, showed up in the Person of the Angel of the LORD— Jesus: "*And the angel of the LORD found her by a fountain of water in the wilderness, by the fountain in the way to Shur*" (Genesis 16:7).

This Messenger of the LORD, who would one day *submit* in love to the cross, enjoined Hagar to submit herself to Sarah. Moses recorded: "*And the angel of the LORD said unto her, Return to thy mistress, and submit thyself under her hands. And the angel of the LORD said unto her, I will multiply your descendants so that they will be too many to count"* (Genesis 16:9–10).

Here is a consistent pattern of the Angel of the LORD. He appears at key salvation moments. He speaks with the voice of God. He makes powerful Divine promises. And He keeps them—always.

After the lifesaving appearance of the Messenger of the Lord, Hagar marveled. Hagar thought, *Have I really* seen God *and lived to tell about it?* She realized that she had seen God in the form of a Man.

The Messenger of the LORD is mentioned fifty-nine times in the Greek and Hebrew Old Testaments; "the Angel of God" eleven times. All total: seventy. You must look carefully. That rather perfect seven-times-ten number for the perfect Messenger of the LORD who saves, pardons, and comforts, is part of the red-letter story of the words of Jesus.

In summary, you have Jesus showing up as God in ancient times, as well as in New Testament times, bestowing mercy upon a hurting humanity. I humbly submit that there should be a red-letter edition of Jesus' words in *both* testaments. Maybe one day. What coherent Christological patterns that would show!

Like the character in the *NCIS* television show, Jethro Gibbs, his rule of 39 states, "I don't believe in *coincidences.*"

Reframed I would like to reword it to say, "I do, however, believe in *Divine patterns!*"

Years ago I read a thoughtful clipping by a person who posed this question: If God became a man, then what might we expect of Him? The gentleman responded:

1. To have an utterly unique entrance into human history.

2. To be without sin.

3. To manifest His supernatural presence in the form of supernatural acts—that is, miracles.

4. To live more perfectly than any human who has ever lived before.

5. To speak the greatest words ever spoken.

6. To have a lasting and universal influence.

7. To satisfy the spiritual hunger in humanity.

8. To overcome humanity's most pervasive and feared enemy—death.

The God-Man Messenger of the LORD in the Old Testament and the Messiah of the New Testament touches each of these bases. They are one and the same Person. Each is worshiped (see Joshua 5:13–15; John 20:28). Each speaks the things of God (see Genesis 18:10; 21; John 10:30; 33; Exodus 23:21; Mark 2:5; Luke 23:34). Each does things only God Himself does (see Exodus 14:13; Genesis 19:24; Exodus 34:6–7; Colossians 1:15–17).

There is something else. This God of all grace who enters time and space, He comes to this place to give God a face. As He does He comes to breathe our poison air, to feel our despair, to reveal intimate care, and to repair...this broken cosmos.

He is not a distant deity.

He is not a god far away from Timbuktu.

He is not remote.

He is the God who shows up—even today.

6

The Lamb Provides a Ram (Genesis 22)

When Jesus told the religious leaders in Jerusalem, "Your father Abraham was delighted to know of My day; he saw it and was glad," the religious leaders had no idea what He meant. Abraham really was glad to see Jesus face-to-face. The promise of the miracle birth of Isaac from Jesus' lips to Abraham's ears brought elation, and Jesus' showing up in the nick of time to save Isaac on Mount Moriah brought ecstasy! Regarding this latter story:

The Lamb would provide a ram (see Genesis 22:10–13).

When you face a sticky wicket, think of the ram in the thicket.

God's only begotten Son would save Abraham's only son.

See the weave the Spirit did conceive!

To appreciate how the Messiah showed up at Mount Moriah in pre–Good Friday fashion, two millennia before He would return to that arena once more, we need to provide some biblical background.

God had been testing Abraham for about fifty years! God had been training him to take Him at His word, however absurd...it might seem to be...on the surface. This is a theme for the life of faith and love: take God at His Word!

When God told Abraham to go to Mount Moriah on a three-day journey, echoes of Easter and reverberations of Good Friday gently fuse. First, why three days? It would be a three-day weekend stay for Jesus in the tomb of Joseph of Arimathea. Second, why Mount Moriah? Moriah would, three hundred years later, become Jerusalem, the future home of the ultimate fulfillment of this story.

Second Chronicles 3:1 reads: *"Then Solomon began to build the house of the Lord in Jerusalem on Mount Moriah, where the Lord had appeared to his father David, at the place that David had prepared on the threshing floor of Ornan the Jebusite."*

Just as the Messenger of the Lord *appeared* to King David, the God who shows up would appear to Abraham on Mount Moriah. Here Abraham would face his most severe test in life. Would he be willing to give back to God what God had first given to him?

God would, in time, near the place of Mount Moriah, give to mankind His greatest gift, His only begotten Son. Would Abraham be able to give God *his* greatest human gift?

From all angles, on the surface, God's request seemed utterly absurd. Only the pagan gods made this kind of request. How would the promise be kept, that from Isaac a family of billions would come forth? And what would *Sarah* think? *Am I losing my mind? What does* this *mean?*

Dr. John Boice believed that Isaac was thirty to thirty-five years old at that time—perhaps even thirty-three! Luther guessed he was twenty years old. I see merit in Boice's calculation. Imagine Isaac, at age thirty-three, being offered up near the spot where Jesus, at age thirty-three, would be offered up for the world? Back then "a lad" could even be forty years old. (See Genesis 48:16.)

Hebrews 11:17–19 reveals that Abraham believed in the resurrection of the dead. He believed that God would raise up his son if that was necessary for God's fulfilling His salvation promises. Even more remarkable, given that Genesis 22 made it clear that Isaac was to be a burnt offering, Abraham had confidence that *from the ashes* God could bring forth life. If the God who showed up had breathed life into the dirt of the land to fashion man, and later breathed life into a dead womb, He could also raise Isaac up from the ashes.

So Abraham concluded.

Martin Luther marveled at the story of Abraham's faith. He wrote, "These events are recorded for our comfort, in order that we may learn to rely on the on the promises that we have... I have stated that Abraham's trial was, namely, the contradiction of the promise."

Read the story for yourself. See how moving it is. Pay close attention to the language of the God who shows up, the Messenger of the LORD. Robert Jenson points out how this Messenger (Angel) "like John's *Logos* is both another than God (the Father) and by virtue of the character of otherness is God":

After this God *tested Abraham.* "Abraham!" God said to him. "Yes," he answered. "Take your *only son Isaac, whom you love,*" He said. "Go to the country of Moriah, and *sacrifice* him there as a burnt offering on one of the hills I will point out to you." Early the next morning Abraham harnessed his donkey. He took two of his servants and his son Isaac with him. He cut the wood for the burnt offering. Then he started out for the place God told him about.

On the third day Abraham looked and saw the place in the distance. Then Abraham said to his servants, "Stay here with the donkey. I and the boy will go over here and worship. Then <u>we'll come back</u> to you." Abraham took the wood for the burnt offering and laid it on his son Isaac while he took the fire and knife in his hands. And both were walking together.

Then Isaac said to his father, "My father." "Yes, my son," he answered. "We have the fire and the wood," said Isaac, "but where is the lamb for the burnt offering?" "God will provide <u>Himself</u> with a lamb for the burnt offering, my son," Abraham answered. And so they both walked on together.

When they came to the place God had mentioned, *Abraham* built the altar there and arranged the wood. Then he bound *his son Isaac* and laid him on the wood *on the altar.* As *Abraham* reached for the knife and took it in his hand to *sacrifice his son,* <u>The Angel of the LORD</u> called to him from heaven, "Abraham! Abraham!" "Yes, he answered."

"Don't lay your hands on the boy," He said, "and don't do anything to him. Now I know you fear God: you didn't refuse to <u>Me</u> your *only son.*"

When Abraham looked around, he saw behind him a ram caught by his horns in a bush. So Abraham went and got the ram and sacrificed him as a burnt offering instead of his son. Abraham called the place THE-LORD-WILL-PRO-VIDE. Today we still say, "On the mount of the LORD it will be provided."

Again the Angel of the LORD called to Abraham from heaven: "*I swear by <u>Myself</u>, says the LORD, because you did this* *and didn't refuse to give up your only son, I will bless you richly and give you many descendants, like the stars in the sky and the sand on the seashore,* and your descendants will capture the city of their enemies. *In your Descendant all the nations on earth will be blessed,* because you have done what I told you" (emphasis mine).

Do you see how the Messenger of the LORD speaks just like God? Verse 15 explicitly identifies the Messenger of the Lord as the LORD. The fact that the rising Messiah appears on Moriah, the future home of Solomon's Temple, providing a ram as the Lamb, weaves together a silhouette for Good Friday and Easter (see 2 Chronicles 3:1). Here God's Temple, Jesus, would be sacrificed, torn down, and raised up (see John 2:19).

Like all believers in Messiah, Abraham was called by the Gospel (see 2 Thessalonians 2:14). The Gospel is the story of salvation that comes to all mankind through the Person and work of Jesus Christ. Through the promised Savior and His merciful love, Abraham was called out of darkness into God's marvelous light. Recall the gifts of grace given to Abraham by the God who shows up:

    A. Called out of the darkness of polytheism (Genesis 12:1–3).

    B. Eternal salvation, the gift of righteousness via the Word and Gospel promise (15:6).

C. Wisdom, the spirit of acquiescence and wisely yielding, being willing to be last in order to be first (Genesis 13:8–13). He gives Lot the best choice of land and Lot is penny-wise, spiritually pound foolish.

D. Courage 14:15).

E. Spiritual blessings: meets Melchizedek (14:9), a type of Christ.

F. Sublime social security (15:15).

G. Forgiveness for shading the truth (20:17).

H. Protection from Sodom and Gomorrah and the grisly lawless men living in that city, men without pity (Genesis 19).

I. The gift of a miracle son (Genesis 21:3) and joy (21:6).

K. The promise of a heavenly city (Hebrews 11:10).

L. A faith in the belief of the resurrection of the dead (Hebrews 11:19).

God showed up to provide Abraham a miracle-born boy (see Genesis 18). He showed up at Mount Moriah to provide a ram, because He Himself would become the Lamb (see John 1:29). The fact that Moriah became Jerusalem 300 years after *Alkeda,* the Jewish name for the binding of Isaac, is also very significant. The fact that Isaac would submit to his father is a powerful prophetic picture of the Messenger of the LORD submitting to His Father to secure our salvation.

A Lamb goes uncomplaining forth, the guilt of sinners bearing.

And laden with the sins of earth, None else the burden sharing;

Goes patient on, grows weak and faint, To slaughter led without complaint,

That spotless life to offer, He bears the stripes the wounds,

the lies, the mockery, and yet replies, "All this I gladly suffer."

This Lamb is Christ, the soul's great friend, The Lamb of God, our Savior,

Whom God the Father chose to send To gain for us His favor.

"Go forth, My Son," the Father said, "And free My children from their dread.

Of guilt and condemnation. The wrath and stripes are hard to bear,

But by Your passion they will share The fruit of your salvation."

Paul Gerhardt, 1607–76,
"A Lamb Goes Uncomplaining Forth"

7

The Jacob-Wrestling God

Have any of you ever wrestled against a *really* good opponent? In college I wrestled in my weight class against the top wrestler in the world. It was my coaches' way to get me ready for a big wrestling tournament in Chicago. "Hey, Pete, I am going to have you scrimmage against someone who is really good!"

Groovy, I thought. That was the "in word" back then. At the time I had no idea that the gentleman was a former Olympic gold medalist. He was twenty-nine years old and I was twenty.

Was he good! He mopped me up. I lost, twelve to one. The only reason I even got that one measly point was because he let me up purposely to take me down to get two more points. In the match he gave me a cross-face move that made me think he had stuck my nose into my eardrum. Fortunately, he was a Christian. Had he wanted to hurt me, I suspect he could have. Until that contest, I thought I was pretty good. That match was a nine-course meal of nothing but humble pie. It confirmed that I should be a pastor, not a wrestler.

Having gone through this experience, it should be no surprise to you that one of my favorite stories in the Bible is the one in which Jacob literally wrestled with God. The grandson of Abraham wrestled with the God who shows up. This is the very God who by a miracle brought Jacob's father into the world. What a strange story! These strange stories continue.

To get our attention, Jesus, in the Old Testament and in the New Testament age, repeatedly stands truth upside on its head. So many Christians look dumbfounded when you tell them that the Bible teaches that Jesus showed up frequently throughout the Old Testament. Yet, these appearances are part of the Gospel story.

In Genesis 32 we have God in the flesh humbling Himself at the River Jabbok and foreshadowing His birth in Bethlehem. Strange, yes. Even eye-popping! Yet commentators and translators are ho-hum about something so spectacular.

A look at some of the various biblical captions, not part of the text, reveal how translators skirt around the reality of the God who shows up. Many of these translations have no caption about such a major theophany—this clear-cut appearance of God! Others introduce an aspect about this stunning story, but they avoid celebrating the obvious. Here are a few of the rather blasé captions:

Jacob Wrestles

Jacob Wrestles at Peniel

Jacob Wrestles with God

Jacob's Fourth Encounter with God—He Wrestles with God

That last caption is excellent. An exclamation mark after it would have been fitting, though! That heading comes from a translation titled "God's Word." Still, it lacks the Christological conclusion that the Holy Spirit beckons believers to draw. It is a conclusion that no doubt Jesus pointed out to the Emmaus disciples after He rose from the dead (see Luke 24).

My caption would read: *Jesus Wrestles with Jacob.*

Why Jesus? Because Jesus is the only Person in the Holy Trinity who in the Bible *appears* in the form of God and man. My suggested caption is the evangelical elephant in the room. Interpreters of all stripes succumb to peer pressure to avoid articulating the obvious: *Jesus wrestles with Jacob.*

Theologians all too often want to keep God at a distance. The "down to earth" God of the Bible who shows up *throughout* the two testaments is a bitter pill for ancient and modern man.

Why is the "down-to-earth" God such a bugaboo for interpreters of the Bible? By nature, humans want to construct a ladder to heaven themselves, so that we climb there by our insights, by our works, by our deeds. The self-flattering, egotistical view of getting to heaven by a ladder truly does flatter. We want to be ladder-day saints.

God coming to Planet Earth punctures our pride. By nature we do *not* want a God who has blood and water pouring from His side. That is why so many churches have abandoned Good Friday services—missing the very point of God's extravagant love!

Gerhard Forde called the theologians who do this revisionism of the text, "God-remodelers" and he says that they "are a dime a dozen." Rather than taking God at face value, they twist the text. This twisting of truth is called "iniquity," and it is a ubiquity when it comes to taking God's Word in a straightforward fashion.

Since context is king in biblical interpretation, some backdrop to the story of Jesus wrestling with Jacob is helpful. When Jacob was born, he came out of his mother's womb hanging on for dear life—clinging to his twin brother's heel. This little cling-on already was manifesting a competitive spirit. Already in Rebekah's womb, Jacob and his brother, Esau, were going at it—a wrestling match between two future nations!

Poor Rebekah! She had two nations in her womb (see Genesis 25:21–23). No wonder she had such a tough pregnancy. Furthermore, even though she gave birth to two boys at once, they went radically different directions in life. This caused Martin Luther to make a keen observation, dubbing astrology as bunk. When asked whether he believed in the superstition that the stars determined one's destiny, Luther grunted, "Jacob and Esau."

In a prophecy, the Lord told Rebekah that the younger son (Jacob) would be served by the older (Esau). (See Genesis 25:33.) Like Sarah and Abraham, Jacob and Rebekah felt they had to help God along. They had to enlist trickery that leads to treachery. First, Jacob swindled Esau out of his birthright (see Genesis 25:29–34). Second, with the help of Rebekah, Jacob tag-teamed to deceive Isaac into giving the firstborn blessing to the second-born son, Jacob (see Genesis 27). Soap opera city!

Esau was so angry over this double swindle that he wanted to murder Jacob. Jacob must run. He fled to the faraway land of his shiftless uncle Laban (see Genesis 27:41–45). There he lived for twenty years, marrying two of Laban's daughters and being blessed with eleven sons. The Lord also blessed Jacob with abundant material blessings (see Genesis 30:43).

Jacob the trickster got two decades of comeuppance via the roguery of Laban. Ten times lusty Laban changed his word when it came to Jacob's wages. Laban in a way was a mirror bright to bring to light Jacob's past con-artist ways.

Well, there is a time and a season for everything. After twenty years, it was finally time for Jacob to return home. He stealthily fled from Laban, taking his family and his flocks. Hotheaded Laban would likely have reduced Jacob to chopped liver, but God protected Jacob. God let Laban know that if he harmed Jacob, God would turn Laban into toast (see Genesis 31:24). Thus, by God's grace and mercy, Jacob survived the first threat on his life.

The Divine drama quickens. Jacob's soul sickens. He feared that an irate, still angry Esau was going to dismantle him. Esau was a mighty warrior, and Jacob was merely a shepherd. This was a major mismatch. Then Jacob learned that Esau was approaching—with 400 soldiers.

With his mind on overdrive, a crafty but fretting Jacob was pacing. It was the night before the scheduled reunion. Jacob was by himself—so he had time to think and fret and sweat. As he was stewing in guilt for having stolen his brother's birthright, he wondered what he would do come showdown time.

That night by the River Jabbok, one of the most mysterious and unexpected events in all of the Bible took place.

The "down-to-earth" God showed up. A mysterious Man appeared out of seemingly nowhere. He began wrestling with Jacob. These two wrestled until dawn.

I can tell you personally that, after eight minutes of a tough match, even a well-conditioned body is spent. Your legs and your limbs feel like cooked spaghetti. Somehow Jacob was given miraculous strength to wrestle against this Superhuman opponent. Pain. Agony. Struggle. Humility. Shades of Gethsemane.

Through the night until dawn, they wrestled. Jacob with the gift of Samson-like strength (see Judges 15:15–16) held his own. When this mysterious Man, who came in a state of humiliation, saw that He could not win against Jacob, He touched the socket of Jacob's hip. With that one touch, Jacob's hip socket became a dislocated sprocket. Extreme pain rifled to Jacob's brain. An agonizing groan filled the air.

In the midst of all of this distress, a light bulb went off in Jacob's mind. He rightly concluded that this mystery Man at any time could have reduced him to ashes. He, Jacob, was the lesser; this Man was the greater.

It is apparent that the mystery Man desired *not* to be *fully* seen by Jacob. Perhaps it was because this Man, seen face-to-face in His *full* glory, might just be an unhealthy sight for any sinner. Jacob did not want to get what he deserved.

Perhaps the later words spoken to Moses apply: "But you can't see my face, because no one may see me and live" (Exodus 32:20). Jacob seeing this Man in His raw glory would end his story. He realized he was wrestling on holy ground.

It was almost *dawn*. At dawn, the great salvation events in the Bible often appear: the splitting of the Red Sea, the Messenger of the LORD taking out 185,000 Assyrian soldiers, and the angel announcement of Jesus being risen (see Exodus 14:24; 2 Kings 19:35; Luke 24:1). In all such scenarios, including the one with Jacob, one Person shows up repeatedly. It is the down-to-earth God. He comes into the world to bless, to save, to free, and to restore.

The Man said, "Let Me go; it is almost dawn."

But Jacob answered, "I won't let you go until You bless me."

The Man asked Jacob, "What's your name?"

"Jacob," he answered.

The Man said, "Your name will no longer be Jacob but **Israel** [He struggles with God], because you have struggled with God and with men—and you won."

Jacob said, "Please tell me Your name."

The man answered, "Why do you ask for My name?" Then He blessed Jacob there. So Jacob named that place

Peniel [the Face of God], because, he said, "*I have seen God face to face, but my life was saved.*"

The sun rose as Jacob passed Peniel (see Genesis 32:26–31).

Jacob, with the bad limp and death-warmed-over appearance, likely looked so bad, that it might have contributed to Esau taking pity on him when he looked at his bedraggled brother.

Jacob realized that by God's grace this mysterious Man with whom he had wrestled was somehow truly God and man. Here is a Christmas warmup. Here is a BC pre-Incarnation celebration, as an adumbration of the Word made flesh Who pitched a tent here on earth for thirty-three years (see John 1:14).

Later in the Old Testament, Hosea beautifully summarized this epic episode. Who was this masked Man? Hosea writes, "When Jacob became a man, he struggled with God. He struggled with the Messenger and won. Jacob cried and pleaded with him. Jacob found him at Bethel and he talked with him there" (Hosea 12:3–5).

After the resurrection of Jesus from the dead and after Pentecost, the disciples of Jesus had an epiphany. They saw how Jesus was showing up throughout all the OT era. Emmaus walks and Scripture talks melded with post-resurrection appearances caused the apostles to recognize

Jesus' divinity, lay hold of the idea of the Trinity, and have an affinity for the Christ-centeredness of the Old Testament (see John 20:28; Matthew 28:16–20; Luke 24:13–35).

Peter would later declare, "*All* the prophets testify that people who believe in the one named Jesus receive forgiveness for their sins through him" (Acts 10:43).

It was this Messenger of God who sustained Jacob during the years under Laban's tyranny, working everything together for good (see Genesis 31:11). It was this same Messenger who would sustain Joseph in his dreams-to-dungeons-to-diadems journey, working everything together for good (see Genesis 50:20). It was this Messenger of the LORD who appeared to Jacob, giving him the same promises of salvation He had first given to Abraham and Isaac (see Genesis 28:10–19).

Striking are the words so similar to those of the Messenger of the LORD who intervened to save Isaac: "I am the Lord, the God of your grandfather Abraham and the God of Isaac. I will give the land on which you are lying to you and your descendants. Your descendants will be like the dust on the earth. You will spread out to the west and to the east, to the north and to the south... Remember I am with you" (Genesis 29:13–15; 22:15–18).

This is Immanuel language.

This is the language of the Messenger of the LORD.

This is the language of the God who repeatedly shows up to bring to people in the Old Testament a message that is merciful and marvelous and Messianic.

8

Again, and Again, and Again...

In 1969 I had a German professor who headed the religion department at the secular university I attended. He was an atheist. This man, though very erudite from a worldly point of view, was biblically challenged. He boasted back then how a man, like God, would one day be able to "create" life. He did not know the difference between "make" and "create." The Hebrew word for *create* in Genesis 1:1 means to "make out of nothing." He didn't know anything about "nothing."

He did not work closely with the biblical languages. That was one problem. Nor did he grasp the deadly fruit of his holocaust-producing theology. He hadn't learned squat about the lethal nature of his no-show god. Moreover, this expert on religion missed the core meaning of the opening verse of the Bible.

Actually what was happening in American universities during the post WWII years was a serpentine, subterfuge change. Many *theology* classes taught in the universities were downgraded to *religion* classes. This was a seismic shift by the social engineers in our society. From the objective Word of God to the subjective word of man to moral wasteland was the plan.

These clandestine changes would pave the way for whatever utopian solution that the power-hungry oligarchy would conjure up to weaken Jesus' gift of the nuclear family. Preach utopia. Produce dystopia.

To help confuse the students even more, the librarians stacked books heavily in favor of a liberal ideology to lessen any chance for a fair, informed debate. A stacked deck of liberal professors plus a stacked deck of radical books did not bode well for supporters of the ideology that had given birth to Lady Liberty.

So much for liberal tolerance.

Thus, rather than studying *theology*, the Word of God, students were forced at academic gunpoint to study *religion*, the words of men. Taxpayer money had to pay for the students' exposure to all kinds of things that fostered the extremes of legalism and lawlessness.

The founders and framers overwhelmingly rejected the no-show-god ideology that gave birth to the French Revolution, its reign of terror, and its extremes. The God who showed up, Jesus of Nazareth, revealed a love to mankind here in time and space that provided the providential mercy for a nation to emerge, guided by self-evident truths. A critical mass of the founders, inspired by the God who showed up and guided by natural law, common law, and biblical law, avoided the extremes of mob-ocracy and theocracy.

They had biblical balance. In general, they went neither too far to the right nor too far to the left (see Deuteronomy 5:32). Except for the compartmentalization of the anti–Golden Rule institution of slavery, they came up with the best government ever launched by men. Had they harvested even better from Leviticus and Jesus' Sermon on the Mount and the message of the cross (see Matthew 27:32), slavery would not have become a bitter, besmirched part of our history (see Leviticus 19:34; Matthew 7:12).

As America made a break from England in 1776, at least fifty years of solid biblical teaching paved the way for the Declaration of Independence. Had the theology of the God who showed up not been taught throughout the thirteen colonies at that time, our Republic would never have been born—for the common thread that ran through the heads of the founders and framers was the rule of law. That rule of law came from the Bible in general, and the book of Deuteronomy in particular. The latter was *abundantly* quoted by the founders. Moses, of course, set forth this good law through the wisdom he received personally from face-to-face conversations with the God who, in veiled form, showed up to be with him (see Deuteronomy 34:10).

The God who showed up to call Moses into action provided the Law and Gospel substance necessary for the birth of our nation. By the balance-beam inspiration of the theology of the cross, the sensibilities to avoid the extremes that other governments swallowed were avoided (see Ephesians 2:8–10). Wherever the message of the cross takes root in a culture, it causes people to recognize the extremes of anarchy and authoritarianism and to eschew them both.

The founders wisely sought to avoid a Church State on the one hand, and the complete separation of Church and State on the other hand. They sought a paradox of functional interaction and institutional separation at the same time. The fumes of the paradoxical theology of the cross provided the ability to live in such wholesome tensions.

All of this was inspired by the God who showed up, who said, "Render unto Caesar the things that are Caesar's and to God the things that are God's!"(Matthew 22:21). Jesus spoke these words around 26 AD. However, it was His visitations to Moses 1,500 years earlier in Exodus that set the stage for the revelation of the self-evident truths that also serve well any nation truly interested in genuine freedom.

To understand how God showed up on Planet Earth 3,500 years ago, we need some biblical background. The children of Israel had been in Egypt for 430 years (see Exodus 12:40). The bulk of these years they dwelt in wretched slavery. Before this time, they had dwindled to a remnant of seventy to seventy-five people. The promise of God first given to Abraham seemed to be hanging by a thread. They were threatened by extermination and amalgamation. How would billions of believers in a coming Messiah arise from this little mustard-seed clan? Yet, it would.

God's strange ways of saving His people is a major theme of the God who shows up. The itty-bitty family brought down by Joseph into Egypt would grow and grow. Through gestation in the womb of Egypt, they would multiply to become a nation of over two million people during their 430 years of slavery. Ironically, the fiery furnace of Egypt provided a warm incubator for God's people to proliferate into a nation that would turn into the twelve tribes of Israel.

Still, these slaves needed a leader. The eternal God who shows up was working on an eighty-year project to prepare the leader necessary to guide the slaves to the Promised Land. A little boy by the name of Moses was born. In order to survive the abortion holocaust campaign of the Egyptian leaders, his parents were moved to build a little ark smeared with asphalt and pitch. They put their three-month-old boy in this basket boat and set him afloat down the Nile (see Exodus 2).

Overseeing the whole project was the God who shows up. He guided that boat, that little ark, to float to a place where Pharaoh's daughter went to bathe. The death waters of the Nile-god were turned into salvation waters by the hand of the Eternal I AM. Moses became adopted—as a grandson of Pharaoh. He received a phenomenal education in the Egyptian universities, which were the Oxford and Cambridge universities of his day. Those who are Egyptology scholars see strong traces of Egyptian language in the first five books of the Bible, as well as mathematical meters that are off the charts.

Although immensely intelligent, well-educated, physically strong, and a man of political clout, Moses blundered badly when he murdered an Egyptian taskmaster. His own people turned against him. Pharaoh got wind of Moses' killing an Egyptian who had struck a Hebrew slave. He tried to kill Moses. Moses fled (see Exodus 2:11–15).

Eventually Moses would encounter seven daughters of the priest of Midian. Moses the Egyptian saved these seven daughters from Midian shepherds who were ruffians. He had no idea that the God who shows up would actually turn this Egyptian into a shepherd so that he would one day lead His people out of Egypt. It is a chiastic picture to foreshadow all the paradoxes of the cross.

Next, God gave Moses a forty-year vicarage in the wilderness, learning patience while tending sheep (see Exodus 2). When Moses was at the age of eighty, the Messenger of the LORD appeared to Moses to commission him to lead His people out of the house of slavery (see Exodus 3). His retirement was put on hold for forty more years.

"Fire, fire, fire, the God of Abraham, Isaac, and Jacob, not the God of the philosophers." Those were the conversion-confessing words of Blaise Pascal on the night the Holy Spirit called him by the Gospel (see 2 Thessalonians 2:14). Surveying all the Bible with his photographic memory, Pascal was moved by the Spirit to choose the image of fire to show how purifying fire shows up wherever the Burning Bush shows up.

Pascal saw the coherence of the down-to-earth God and used this metaphor to confess that Jesus is Lord. Whether to Moses in Exodus 3, to Gideon in Judges 6, to Elijah in 1 Kings 19, or to Shadrach, Meshach, and Abednego in the fiery furnace in Daniel 3, the God who shows up comes with a Pentecost-purifying fire (see Acts 2). Such fire was to signify salvation, restoration, and sanctification, and much more.

It was a majestic, Messianic sight when the Messenger of the LORD showed up on the mountain to call Moses into service. *"The Angel of the LORD appeared to him in flames of fire* coming out *of a bush."* He saw the bush *burning* without it being burned up. "I am going over there," Moses said, "to see this wonderful sight. Why doesn't the bush burn up?" (see Exodus 3:2–3).

Reverently Moses approached the burning bush. As he drew nearer, God called out to him from the bush, "Moses, Moses!"

"Yes," Moses answered.

"Don't come any nearer," *He said. "Take your sandals off your feet, because you are standing on holy ground."* Then He said, *"I am the God of your father, the God of Abraham, the God of Isaac, and the God of Jacob."* Moses hid his face, because *"he was afraid to look at God"* (see Exodus 3:4–6).

The words *"Take your sandals off your feet, because you are standing on holy ground"* are in essence the very words Jesus also spoke to Joshua forty years later. It was just before Joshua was slated to lead Israel to conquer Jericho . Then Jesus, as the Captain of the Lord's Army, or the Captain of the Angel Armies, the LORD of hosts, *appeared* (see Joshua 5:14).

The God who shows up *appeared* at the burning bush, as well as on the outskirts of Jericho. He is the Alpha and Omega, not bound by time and space. In both instances, Moses and Joshua fell to the ground and worshiped the Messenger of the Lord (see Exodus 3:5–6; Joshua 5:14). Jesus' great commission to Moses and Joshua ran the same way.

Divine Déjà Vu.

Joshua was visited by JOSHUA, the ONE whose name means "SALVATION." It is this ONE who would bring SALVATION to the whole wide world (see 2 Corinthians 5:19–21). Moreover, Moses revealed that this almighty Messenger of the Lord also pardoned sins! (see Exodus 23:20–23; Mark 2:7). He walked like God. Talked like God. Did the things of God!

What a wonderful weave by Him whose name means "Wonderful!" (Isaiah 9:6). The Holy Spirit kept heaping Divine names and revealing Divine deeds of this Messenger of the LORD, the Captain of the Angel Armies, this Angel of God (see Exodus 14:19), this Divine Wrestler (see Genesis 32), this Being who spoke like God, who rained bread from heaven in 1500 BC, who fed in *ex-nihilo* fashion thousands around 26 AD.

Saint Paul met Him face-to-face on the road to Damascus, this same God who shows up (see Acts 9). When he did, Saul was stunned to see how far short human works come when it comes to saving man. At the end of his life, while in a Philippian jail cell, Saul, who became Paul, which means "small," wrote about how short human works were in terms of a ladder to heaven. The English translations of Philippians 3:8 describe human works as "rubbish" and "garbage" when used as a ticket to heaven.

The Greek, however, is much stronger. It uses the word *skubbala*. This is a loaded word for what you would step in in a well-populated cow pasture. He wanted the Philippians to have a mature faith, not a manure faith. Whether to Moses at Sinai, to Joshua at Jericho, or to Paul on the Damascus Road, the message was, "Take your shoes off in God's presence."

Human works don't cut it. Only the perfect works of the God who shows up on our behalf will open the gate to heaven. Blessedly, His perfect record is *a gift* from God through the gift of faith through the gift of His pardoning love. Trying to work one's way to heaven is a double insult. It implies Jesus is a semi-savior, not Lord. It also implies that we can bribe our way into heaven with cow-pie works wrapped up in filthy, stench-stinking rags (see Philippians 3:8; Isaiah 64:6).

What I am setting forth is no new doctrine. Martin Luther and John Gerhard, two Lutheran theologians, set forth this same good news. Luther, especially in his last commentaries on the book of Genesis, saw clearly how the Messenger of the LORD was Jesus. Gerhard came to a similar conclusion writing, *"When either the name Yahweh (the Lord) or divine works or divine worship is attributed in Scripture to an angel, then this Angel must be understood to be the Son of God."*

Gerhard was considered the greatest Hebrew scholar in Europe in his day.

Early Church fathers also testified similarly. Justin Martyr declared, *"Our Christ conversed with Moses out of the bush, in the appearance of fire. And Moses received great strength from Christ, who spake to him in the appearance of fire"* (ca. AD 150).

Irenaeus, another early Church father, saw how Jesus was the God who showed up in the Old Testament era as well as the New Testament times. Writing around 180 AD, he commented on the BC appearances of the Word made flesh. He wrote, *"The Scripture is full of the Son of God appearing: sometimes to talk and eat with Abraham, at other times to instruct Noah about the measures of the ark; at another time to seek Adam; at another time to bring down judgment upon Sodom; then again, to direct Jacob in the way; and again, to converse with Moses out the bush."*

The God who shows up we again see in Exodus splitting the Red Sea, saving His people by water and the Word. In Exodus 14, we have Pharaoh sending out his mighty forces to wipe out the Israelites. His pyramids had been built on the bloody backs of the children of Israel to foreshadow how Jesus, Israel reduced to One, would have His back bloodied on the altar of the cross to free mankind.

With pathological madness and hellish hubris, Pharaoh took off like a bat out of hell after the children of Israel. Moses and the children of Israel were camped by the Red Sea with the waters to their back. With Pharaoh pursuing them like a rabid crocodile on steroids, Moses saw that from a human point of view, Israel was facing a full massacre. The people, in full panic, manic mode, wanted to lynch Moses and go back to slavery...typical of humans preferring slavery and security to freedom and responsibility.

As Pharaoh barreled down upon the Israelites, Moses offered up a prayer. He told the Israelites, "Don't be afraid! Stand still and see what the LORD will do to *save (Jesus)* you today. You will never see these Egyptians again. The LORD is fighting for you! So be still and know!"

A paraphrase of this powerful passage where the name of Jesus is nestled is, "Stand back and see Jesus at work!" (see Exodus 14:13). If there was any doubt about Jesus being present, verse 19 eliminates it by illuminating with more burning bush clarity:

"The Messenger of God, who had been in front of the Israelites, moved behind them. So the column of smoke moved from in front of the Israelites and stood behind, between the Egyptian camp and the Israelite camp."

Next, the Spirit-strong wind from the east drove the waters back. Psalm 35 tells how the Messenger of the Lord brought about Divine entrapment to save the vulnerable (see Exodus 35:4–5). His holy wrath for the sake of saving the poor in Spirit was about to manifest itself in strange ways. Just as Jesus saves by water with resurrection power today (see 1 Peter 3:21), Yeshua was going to save by water with salvation power then. Through this powerful Red Sea baptism, Jesus saved (see 1 Corinthians 10:2) through the Rock that was Christ (see 1 Corinthians 10:4).

In one day, the Messenger of the LORD created a nation. In one day He took down the greatest slave-holder nation. In one day, He who would walk on water recruited water not only to save God's people, but to drown hard-hearted Pharaoh and all his hosts in the Red Sea. The LORD of hosts drowned Pharaoh and all his hosts in order to free the oppressed and to preserve the powerful Messiah promises He first gave to Adam in the Garden (see Genesis 3:15).

Again, and again, and again, and again, the God of all grace shows up!

9

Other Old Testament Appearances

W e have seen clear references of God showing up in Genesis, Exodus, Joshua, and in other places in the Bible. The overall profile as we put the pieces together looks like Jesus. This Person who was worshiped by Moses and Joshua also helped the helpless, brought forgiveness, saved by water, redeemed, performed miracles, and more.

This Messenger of the LORD also had a sense of humor. In the New Testament we see Jesus manifesting a sense of humor, especially in the Sermon on the Mount. He told people not to blow their own horns: "So when you give to the poor don't blow your horn, as hypocrites do in the synagogues and on the streets to be praised by people" (Matthew 6:2).

In addressing the wrong kind of judging versus the right kind of judging, Jesus evinces wit with humor: "Why do you look at the speck in your brother's eye and don't notice the log in your own eye?" (Matthew 7:2). A little later He spoke of not throwing *pearls to pigs*. Beyond the Sermon on the Mount, in Matthew He warned about the malady of straining gnats and swallowing camels—a metaphor that was humorous and memorable (see Matthew 23:24).

Does the God who shows up on Planet Earth have a sense of humor in the Old Testament? The Divine Comedy in Numbers 22:21-38 says "yes." It is the story of how the almighty God caused a donkey to speak to make a false prophet look like a jackass—among other things.

This holy, earthy humor shows a balanced view of God in the flesh. On the one hand, Jesus is the ultimate Man of sorrows, deeply acquainted with grief (see Isaiah 53:3; Matthew 23:37-39; Hebrews 4:14-16). On the other hand, Jesus' sharp mind reflected what the psalmist declared, namely, how the Lord laughs at the wicked (see Psalm 37:13; 2:4).

We plan, God laughs. That's how a fine Yiddish proverb goes. It catches a lot of theological turf. Martin Luther felt that sanctified laughter was a gift from God, and there would be plenty of it in heaven. G.K. Chesterton was of that school, as well.

Back to our story.

Israel had had a series of battles with the cutthroat Canaanites, the murderous Moabites, and the amoral Amorites. A king by the name of Balak was on the rise. Undoubtedly, he had heard about the God who took down Egypt. It was the story of the century. Drowning the most powerful military juggernaut in the ancient world created a historical hiatus in ancient Near East annals. Not much would be written about it. The story was severe law to Egypt but saving gospel to call to faith a prostitute by the name of Rahab. By grace through faith in Christ, Rahab became a future ancestor of King David and the God who shows up (see Matthew 1:5; 1:17–18).

Balak knew that militarily, on papyri, he was a good match against the larger but unseasoned forces of Israel. However, if their God got into the picture, well, *that* would change everything. Egypt's Red Sea ending was Balak's reason for enlisting demonic help.

So, how would Balak neutralize Yahweh, the God of all grace?

To even the playing field, Balak sought a famous prophet for hire. He asked a man named Balaam to put calamity from hell upon God's people. After this overture by Balak, God *came* to Balaam and said, "You are not to curse this people, namely the Israelites, for they are blessed" (Numbers 22:12).

More sweeping in scope, God was trying to save lives on both sides—the innocent who were so easily turned into cheap collateral by the lusty leaders looking for power, prestige, and pageantry. The industrial military complex has been an age-old problem since the Fall. The God of all grace who would one day die on the cross *for all* wanted to protect His people from the big little bully Balak, as well as protect all involved. That was part of the big picture, along with protecting the Remnant from whom would come the Savior of the world.

Balaam, after this sobering encounter with God, told Balak's emissaries "no deal." Balaam had heard about Egypt's end and the universe's beginning—made out of nothing—each compliments of Yahweh. He knew, at least publicly, "You don't tug on Superman's cape."

But Balak would not take no for an answer. He sweetened the offer considerably. More money. More honor. More everything. The hocus-pocus focus of Balaam's demonic wizardry Balak coveted.

Hmmm. Balaam's sinful flesh bit. He was looking for a loophole. How could he outmaneuver a God who knows all things, is all-powerful, and fills the whole universe? On the outside Balaam was playing the part of obedience toward God, but inwardly he was running greedily toward the loot (see Jude 11).

In mercy, God *came* to Balaam once more at night. He let the conflicted prophet know that He knew everything. He said: "Since these men have come to summon you, get up and go with them, but *you must only do what I tell you*" (Numbers 22:20).

Look at the golden calf too long and you grow stupid. *Stupid is as stupid does*, said the philosopher Forrest Gump. Balaam should have cut his losses. Instead, he rode on like a drunken cowboy.

The Lord who searches the heart was totally aware of the selfish soul of the mulish prophet. He saw before what happened how the rebel riding his donkey for a pot of filthy lucre was willing to do this at the expense of the death of innocent people. God was not pleased with the calloused Balaam nor the cutthroat Balak.

As Balaam rode his donkey, the Messenger of the LORD showed up. Jesus here performed an Emmaus Road miracle of sorts. It was like the one He would perform 1,500 years later after He rose bodily from the dead. As Lord of the impossible, Jesus kept Balaam from seeing Him, just as He later closed the eyes of Cleopas and his friend (see Luke 24:13–35).

When the donkey saw the Angel of the LORD standing on the road with His drawn sword in His hand, the donkey turned off the road and went into the field. Smart donkey.

Stupid prophet. Blinded by greed, the piggish prophet couldn't pick up the palpable signs God was giving to him via nature. He did not listen to God's Word. Now he was refusing to listen to the nuances of nature from nature's God.

Peeved Balaam did what humans are so prone to doing—he scapegoated. He scapegoated a donkey. He beat the poor creature, attempting to force it to get back on the road. That is a picture of what all salvation-by-works religions do. Rather than wooing by love, they beat people with lame laws—often arbitrary and burdensome to force people to follow the woeful whims of their nonexistent gods (see 1 Corinthians 8:4).

As the omnipresent Angel of the LORD *appeared*, He stood on a narrow path between vineyards where there was a wall on each side. Seeing the mighty Messenger of the LORD, the donkey pressed against the wall. As the donkey did this, he squeezed Balaam's foot against it. So Balaam, thinking with his bowels rather than his brains, beat the donkey once more.

The God who controls *every* molecule in the universe, the Messenger of the LORD, now stood in a narrow place where there was no room to turn to the right or the left (see Colossians 1:15–17). When the donkey saw the Messenger of the LORD, she lay down. Balaam now lost it! The unrighteous prophet whacked this beast that was simply being obedient to its Lord. This animal was a kindred creature to the obedient Palm Sunday donkey on which our Lord rode into Jerusalem upon (see Proverbs 12:10).

Then the same Lord who created out of nothing billions of light-years in less than a split second, the same Lord who would turn water into wine, nonchalantly gave the donkey the ability to speak. And she, the donkey, asked boneheaded Balaam, "What did I do to you that you should hit me three times?"

"You mocked me! You made me a king-sized fool!" Balaam fumed, totally beside himself. Discombobulated, he exclaimed, "If I had a sword in my hand, I would kill you *right now*!" I am tempted to wish that the donkey had then said, "Those who take the sword will perish with the sword." Jesus could have placed those words then and there in the mouth of the donkey, but He was saving them for a more poignant moment in history (see Matthew 26:52).

"Am I not your donkey," the donkey asked Balaam, "that you have always ridden till today? Have I been in the habit of doing this to you?"

So much had Balaam's lust for money, and his anger for not being in control of a donkey, squeezed his pee-little brain, that he glossed over the obvious. Unrighteous anger so often does this. It causes people to lose all sense of proportion. He who pretended to control the destinies of nations, Balaam, couldn't even handle his own donkey.

Now the donkey was lecturing the devil's point-man!

"No," Balaam answered—taking the donkey's rebuke on the chin.

Then the same Lord who closed the eyes of the Emmaus disciples so that they would see Him in faith through His Word, opened the eyes of the false prophet, Balaam, so that His Word might be received with an open mind. When Balaam saw the Messenger of the LORD standing on the road with His drawn sword, his legs became rubber, his lips blubber, as he did discover what was going on *beyond* the five senses.

Balaam bowed down with his face to the ground. He worshiped at the feet of the same One about whom Thomas confessed, "my God and my Lord" (John 20:28). At that moment, he was feeling like Moses at the Burning Bush and Joshua at Jericho when the Messenger of the LORD showed up. Balaam understood he was on holy *ground.* He was in the presence of the *Ground of all Being.*

Jesus spoke.

"Why did you strike your donkey these *three* times? You see, I came out and appeared to oppose you, because you're going in an evil direction. The donkey saw **Me** and turned away from **Me** these *three* times. If she had not turned away from **Me**, I would have killed you for working toward the murder of My people. But the donkey, I would have kept her alive."

The context of a text is crucial to an enlightening translation. Context is king. Culture is queen. Human reason is the wild card. Not taking God at face value is the joker. By taking context as king, i.e., Balaam worshiping the Messenger, as did Moses and Joshua, the word "**Me**" is rightly, spritely capitalized, as did William Beck render it in the above translation.

Balaam was overwhelmed by the presence of God in the flesh. To be sure, it was Jesus in veiled form *because* no human can stand before God on earth when the heaviness of His full glory is manifested. Jesus is the Rock of Ages, the Cleft for us, the Divine Shield to protect us till we are fully formed in glory (see Galatians 2:20). Balaam told the Angel of the LORD, "I have sinned! I didn't know You were standing on the road opposing me. And now, if You don't like this, I'll go back" (v. 34. Beck).

"Go with the men," the Angel of the LORD told Balaam, "but say only what I tell you."

"So Balaam went with Balak's princes" (v. 35 Beck).

The way God shows up as God and man has irritated skeptics living in a pre-Einstein universe. You have these finite men judging the storytelling ways of the greatest

Teacher who ever walked on earth, One who is not bound by time and space. They foolishly lecture God. The LORD is not permitted to bring about a very good story for the sake of a larger salvation story? Give me a break.

Think about it. God has a wide, millenniums-old audience. It is marked by an acute need to learn of God through oral culture stories anchored in history, revealing Himself in strange memorable stories. Also, God must deliver at the same time material that is simultaneously milk of the Word and meat of the Word. Someone has said it well: *"If God were to explain to us the simplest mysteries of the universe, it would be like Albert Einstein trying to explain to a rock neck crab the theory of relativity."*

Moreover, the God who shows up is delighted by our childlike faith. In God's sight, faith is so precious. Why? When well-anchored, it is linked with *agape* love. Without such faith and love, people cannot be *fully* human.

Amazingly, when Jesus lovingly went to the cross to atone for our sins, He not only was fulfilling prophecy as David's Son and David's Lord (see Psalm 110:1; 22:1), but He was with cosmic precision willing Himself to die at the exact moment when the Passover Lamb was in the temple being slain. This we noted earlier and we note here again. At that moment, the thick temple curtain with the embroidered constellation of stars would rip open. Isaiah 64:1 would be dramatically fulfilled. The graves around

Jerusalem would break open; the Valley of Dry Bones prophecy of Ezekiel would be fulfilled (see Ezekiel 37).

All of this is so strange. It makes this narrative of a talking donkey seem congruently tame, consistently in step with God's strange ways from Noah's ark, to the splitting of the Red Sea, to the walls of Jericho coming down, to Jesus appearing in a fiery furnace, and ultimately to Jesus dying on the cross to atone for the sins of mankind.

Moreover, it is the only profound salvation story in history that has moved humanity toward real progress, real peace, and real freedom. It works. It really works. Shouldn't holy pragmatism count for something?

To a pre-Guttenberg age, God's intervention in history, in Jesus as the Way coming in the BC era, makes sanctified sense. The vast majority of people in BC times did not have access to books and Bibles as we do. Most people could not even read. An unusual striking story would be the normal, loving means to take for the Person who told the greatest stories ever.

From the splitting of the Red Sea to a talking donkey to a prophet being swallowed by a fish to bring good news for all people, the God who comes down uses marvelous means for self-disclosure. He didn't come just for the literate and Gnostic elites, but in kindness Jesus came for *all* people.

Let God be God...His ways seem so odd...yet without this peculiar Gospel element for belief, there is no relief to turn our whoring, warring world toward love and healthy tolerance. Only in the story of the God who shows up do humans have the story of God's intimate, infinite, impressive love. Apart from this awesome news, humans are ever struggling in the quicksand of salvation by works or the quagmire of lawlessness. These are the two extremes that turn people into slaves. They are the main melancholy markers of our present secular age.

10

Overlooked!

There is a propensity for the immensity of our density to cause our minds to miss that which God clearly reveals via His Word. We get distracted so easily. Preconceived notions about God, as if He works in a closed universe where miracles are impossible, cause people to miss an exquisite theological tapestry. It causes them also to miss His intricate imprints upon creation.

Recently a group of scientists declared that the human hand is so majestic that its ability and dexterity necessitates both a Creator and a miracle. Still, many scientists stuck in Darwinian drivel can't swivel. They are unable to take into their system the intricate patterns that beckon one to say, as did Einstein, that "God does not roll dice."

All of this creates treason to reason! Massive unintended consequences occur when natural law is dumped for the law of the jungle. Where this happens, humans cannot even rise to the level of organized selfishness—the basic level necessary for liberty to survive. Feelings flog facts. Ideologies open to healthy pragmatism are despised. Abysmal failures of the past are touted as hope for tomorrow.

The rejection of the God who shows up for a blob god is the new postmodern norm. Keep god gooey, unformed, and unhistorical. This new norm produces abnormal behavior. Bad creeds produce bad deeds, as well as the inability to recognize self-evident truths.

It also diminishes the desire to work for the common-wealth with a Golden Rule flavor. It grossly confuses Einstein's theory of relativity with Frankenstein's moral relativism. The latter disciples do not see that the loss of *veritas* leads to the loss of virtue. How Satan blinds!

No-show gods are only able to produce lukewarm love, not Luke's warm love generated from the pardoning love of Jesus Christ as the Savior of the world. His Gospel for the underdog moves people not to treat people like dogs, but as precious beings (see Luke 23:43). The Gospel of the God who shows up produces a beautiful, profound peacemaking love. It builds hospitals, creates goodwill, and engenders hospitality. It heightens altruism like nothing else.

To see the ever-sad end of a secular society gone amok, another Old Testament story will serve us well. It is the story of a vicious nation wanting to devour a vulnerable nation. Allow me to cite a biblical witness that involves the Messenger of the LORD that scholars give severe short shrift. The story, all about the King of kings, comes from 2 Kings 19.

The context? Assyrian King Sennacherib, a mouthy egotist, defies the Lord God of Israel with his eighth-century BC "smack talk." Assyrian kings were known for their ruthlessness. They would fillet the skin off of people—alive—if the preyed upon tried to resist their oppression. They would put hooks into the noses of those who were led off to captivity. They treated humans in sub-human fashion (see 2 Kings 19).

King Sennacherib's goal not only was to advance by cruelty his kingdom of hate, but it was also to destroy God's Kingdom of love. Behind the surface, the geopolitical implications of King Hezekiah's day created a raging cosmic battle. Sennacherib, the Stalin of his day, was one more useful idiot of the devil. Of him and them, Jesus said such individuals in service of Satan "come only to steal and kill and destroy. I came so that people might have life and have it overflowing in them" (John 10:10).

Liberal intellectuals and skeptics of the Bible often object over God commanding Israel in Joshua and Moses' day to kill every man, woman, and child of supremely lawless nations (see Deuteronomy 20:16–17; Joshua 20:16–17).This command came on the heels of four hundred years of patience, where God gave the lawless and loveless every opportunity to turn away from evil. Egypt's crash should have awaken them.

Instead, for forty more years, these people continued to burn children alive and have sex with animals. Their extreme lawlessness made the land of Palestine putrid. The land itself was ready to vomit them up (see Leviticus 18:21–28).

In ancient days, when God's cup of wrath was full, the Angel of the LORD led in the taking out of those who burnt babies alive, committed bestiality, fostered sex trafficking, promoted kidnapping and slavery, and engaged in all kinds of unnatural acts (see Exodus 23:20–23).

Often critics of the Bible today consistently favor supporting cruel predators over protecting the innocent vulnerable. Part of this is due to a sloppy, piecemeal reading of the Bible. The other part is due to the fact that some of today's critics believe it is all right to engage in such lawless behavior. Most of them have never been on the end of the cruel treatment they blithely defend. They lack sympathy and empathy. They are low on love, paltry on pity.

Just as the Gospel of Luke is the Gospel for underdogs, God is always enjoining His baptized children of love to speak out in behalf of the vulnerable and marginalized (see Proverbs 31:8–9). The record of the *loyal* followers of the God who shows up is one of compassion for the down-and-out and advocacy for the oppressed.

In the Old Testament, it is the Messenger of the LORD, Jesus, who drowns hardhearted Pharaoh and his henchmen in order to free the oppressed (see Exodus 12:23; 14:13; 19). He takes out the whole army of the most mighty military juggernaut in its day. This is the same One who drove out of the temple the cruel money merchants.

These greedy, seedy religious folks were oppressing the people, forcing them to buy their price-gouged sacrifices. They were in essence putting a price tag on the free gift of forgiveness, running their own indulgences scam. Jesus was not pleased with this extensive moneymaking racket. It turned Abraham's salvation-by-grace God into a pagan salvation-by-works deity. When Jesus cleansed the temple, He cut into the profit of nine thousand priests involved in this web of wickedness.

Coming back to 2 Kings 19, Judah's back was against the wall, just as was Israel's when Pharaoh and his elite forces were bearing down upon them. Sennacherib's army was waiting for the signal to wipe out God's people. This wicked king had no idea that the same Messenger of the LORD who took down the predators of Sodom and Gomorrah and the tyrants of Egypt was about to devour these devourers. Here is the culmination point from Scripture:

"Then something happened that night—totally unexpected. The Messenger of the LORD went out in the camp of the Assyrians and killed 185,000, and when people got up in the **morning,** they saw all the dead bodies" (2 Kings 19:35).

It was in the *morning* that the Messenger of the LORD blessed Jacob with the new name of "Israel." It was in the *morning* that the Messenger of the LORD destroyed Pharaoh and his army. It was in the *morning* that the Messenger of the LORD sent angels to proclaim that He had risen from the dead on the third day. And it was in the *morning* that the Messenger of the LORD unveiled His act of love and rescue to His people under King Hezekiah. He killed those planning mayhem and murder. He saved the weak and vulnerable from the amoral Assyrians. Justice was served for the sake of the Gospel.

Psalm 46 is the outgrowth of the Messenger of the LORD's taking out the major monster of the day. It is a huge salvation story. In Hebrew, often the punch line, the power line of a psalm, is in the Messianic *middle*. In Greek, the force of meaning of a sentence tends to reside at the beginning or end of a sentence. Observing this language clue, we read this "Morning Has Broken" psalm in light of these realities and verities:

Psalm 46

*God is our Refuge and Strength, our very great Help in time of
trouble.*

Thus, we are not afraid even though the earth quakes,

>*even though the mountains topple into the sea;*

>*even though its waters roar and foam,*

>*even though the mountains shake in the middle of it.*

*There is a river whose streams delight God's city, the holy place
where the most high God lives.*

God is in the city—she cannot fall.

GOD WILL HELP HER WHEN THE *MORNING DAWNS!*

*Nations are in confusion and kingdoms totter—when God utters
His voice, the earth trembles.*

The Lord *of the Angel Armies is with us; the Jacob-Wrestling
God is our Refuge.*

Come, see the saving works of the Lord, *what awesome things
He does in the world!*

*He stops wars all over the earth, smashing bows, cutting off
spears, and burning chariots.*

*Stop and realize that I am God! I am high over the nations,
exalted over the world!"*

The Lord *of the Angel Armies is with us; the Jacob Wrestling
God is our Refuge!*

Unfortunately, this salvation story in 2 Kings 19 is passed over with no connection to the similar stealthlike way Jesus weakened Pharaoh's grip upon His people: "At midnight the LORD struck down every firstborn in Egypt from the sons of Pharaoh sitting on his throne to the son of the prisoner in the dungeon and also every firstborn of the cattle" (Exodus 12:29). Where believing Egyptians smeared blood on their doorposts, the Messenger of the LORD provided a way of escape. It is His nature. In time, Jesus would die on a cross for *all*.

Just as the LORD Jesus took mercy on Rahab, the prostitute who would embrace justification by grace through faith in Jesus apart from the works of the law, so was God consistently in the Old Testament open to all who believed in His promises. Wherever cross signs of blood were smeared, grace appeared. The blood of the Lamb of God who takes away the sin of the cosmos was at work, yes, even in the homes of Egyptians—Egyptians and Israelites alike (see Exodus 12:13, 48).

In our Lutheran circles, even among orthodox Lutherans, the Messenger of the LORD text in 2 Kings 19:35 is often reduced to a mere created angel coming to rescue God's people. Not so! Powerful Christology is exchanged for lesser angelology. It is usually not a malicious mistake, just an injudicious take. The Bible records that it was the Angel of the LORD. It was the God who shows up, the Messenger of the LORD (2 Kings 19:35). The psalmist caught this. Twice he exclaimed in Psalm 46, "the Jacob Wrestling God is our Refuge!" As he did, he hearkened back to Genesis 32:22–32 and to 2 Kings 19:35.

Thus we have another stunning salvation story. The Commander of the Lord's Angel Armies (Joshua 5:13–15) shows up once again to protect the Messianic Seed (Galatians 3:26–29) of His future Bride, the Church (Ephesians 5:21–32). As He shows up, He takes out the whole Assyrian army, just as He took out the whole Egyptian military eight centuries before.

His grand design is to comfort the afflicted and afflict the comfortable. Here, the cruel, callous, and cutthroat people with designs to destroy and devour the Remnant of God encountered a day of reckoning. God is loving and holy, and His love is holy-loving. God took out the genocide nation wishing to commit mass murder. For this, the liberal critics and skeptics often cry foul.

This is a twisted judgment.

The Hebrew word for *twisted* sins, *avon,* is often rendered in English as *iniquity. Twisted* describes the thinking of critics of the Bible. They paint the God of love as evil when He brings down the hammer of the law upon perverted predators. Thus, they condone evil in favor of mercy for the oppressed.

Progressive thought is so often code language for failed ideologies of the past. It calls evil good and good evil. We even have progressives today who believe that the way to save the world is to destroy by genocide 6.5 billion people, so that they and rest of the 500 million survivors can live happily ever after. Here is more warped thinking by the same critics who rip God for taking out thugs to protect the innocent! Obviously, too much hemp is being sold and too little of God's love and rescue story is being read.

In summary, the God who shows up does not show up only in the New Testament but also throughout the Old Testament. All of this is a powerful prelude and parallel for and to the Incarnation birth through the Virgin Mary. The Incarnation was both foreshadowed and foretold. It was foreshadowed by the explicit appearances of the God-man in the Old Testament and it was foretold in Isaiah.

Isaiah 7:14 is the precisely pinpointed Jesus prophecy of the *virgin* birth. Here, too, the progressives attempt to make murky a clear text. They excel at obscuring. The Jewish Greek Old Testament rendering of the Hebrew in Isaiah 7:14 is that a virgin (*parthenos*) will conceive and have a son, and His name will be Immanuel [God-Is-With-Us]! That 200 BC Greek translation of the 600 BC Hebrew prophecy is a historical printed miracle. The scholars who reject it prefer living as erudite cavemen abiding in the dark shadows of a closed universe.

It takes so much faith to be an unbeliever. No wonder C.S. Lewis said that hell is the only place where the door is locked from the inside. The poisoned presupposition that miracles must be ruled out in studying the Bible has led astray millions of people, causing them to miss the majestic footprints of the God of all grace. Dr. John Warwick Montgomery's observation is apt:

For us, unlike people of the Newtonian epoch, the universe is no longer a tight, safe, predictable playing field in which we know all the rules. Since Einstein, no modern has had the right to rule out the possibility of events because of prior knowledge of "natural law." The only way we can know whether an event can occur is to whether in fact it has occurred. The problem of "miracles," then, must be solved in the realm of historical investigation, not in the realm of philosophical speculation (*History, Law and Christianity*, p. 41).

Skeptical scholars today are like the Sadducees of Jesus' day. The historical appearances of God in the flesh recorded in the Old Testament were missed and dismissed. Why? Jesus told them, "You don't know the Old Testament Scriptures or God's power" (Matthew 22:29).

How would the religious leaders respond to the God who showed up during His thirty-three-year sojourn on earth as the Messiah born of Mary? Would they treat Jesus in the shabby way that most of the prophets of old had been treated? Jeremiah was imprisoned, Amos was threatened, Elijah was hunted down, and Isaiah was sawn in two.

Before the universe was created, God knew the religious leaders would join with the Roman rulers and arrest the Messenger of the LORD. Due process of law would be tossed aside. By bribes and lies and intimidation, the ruling religious leaders would seek the unjust death of the Messenger of the LORD. Seven unfair trials would take place within a twenty-four-hour period of time by people, Romans and Jews, who prided themselves on due process. The One before whom Joshua and Moses and Gideon bowed and worshiped, the religious leaders would mock and crucify. This and more was *all* foretold in Isaiah 52:13–53:12. Once again, more written miracles!

It is all a very tight, taut weave that God did conceive in love, in Christ, before the foundation of the universe (see Ephesians 1:3–5). This plan involving the God-man (see Colossians 2:9) was carried out flawlessly down to the *exact* second. At the ninth hour we see its power when He refused to drink the sour...wine of men...on a skull-shaped hill called Golgotha—the place of the *skull*. At 3:00 p.m. the eternal God died!

This strange word, *Golgotha*, was placed by the Holy Spirit already back in Exodus 16:16. Moses, by the command of God, told the Israelites to give to each of the *skulls* in the tent this bread that came down from heaven. Now flash-forward 1,500 years. The Bread of Life on Good Friday was on a cross on a skull-shaped hill feeding the world with love so Divine. On that cross, in extreme pain and agony, the Bread of Life prayed for His enemies, *"Father, forgive them for they know not what they do."* That prayer melted the heart of a corrupt son of Abraham hanging on a cross next to Him. Jesus as a Great High Priest, is both the sacrificial victim and the priest manifesting an unconditional love for all mankind on this skull-shaped hill not far from Mount Moriah, where Abraham was willing to sacrifice his only son.

Ultimate salvation would not come by force, but through faith. Jesus would drink the cup of suffering for every human who ever lived. The writer in the New Testament declares, *"He suffered death in order by God's grace to taste death for everyone"* (Hebrews 2:9). Jesus eliminated the Assyrian soldiers in the eighth century BC so that He could come into the world, born of the Virgin Mary, and eliminate for mankind history's greatest existential enemies. Through His death upon the cross, Jesus would cross out sin, reveal God's saving love, and cross up the devil, creating a stunning reversal as a rehearsal for the birth of hope:

Forbid it, Lord, that I should boast.

Save in the death of Christ, my God;

All the vain things that charm me most,

I sacrifice them to His blood.

—*"When I Survey the Wondrous Cross," verse 2*

11

Bringing It All Together

S o, Jesus shows up throughout the Old Testament. He also shows up in the New Testament era. He is the one God who shows up throughout history. Added to this, He is the most positive difference-Maker in the world. He is light-years ahead of anyone else!

In both testaments, He performed mighty miracles. In both He is worshiped. In both He forgives sins. In both He protects the vulnerable, the underdog, the Remnant. The latter He does for the sake of the salvation of all mankind. He splits the Red Sea, stills the storm, walks on water, changes water into wine, and creates all the water in the very beginning.

His Sermon on the Mount is the most profound treatment on love ever penned. His parables provide insight that is memorable and marvelous, always steering between the extremes of legalism and lawlessness. The Old Testament prophecies are empty without His coming, but they are written miracles to behold as we witness the New Testament. His love made known from the cross is by far and away the most dynamic force for altruism in history. His Kingdom and His followers are the largest statistical success story in history. Even history's calendar—of BC and AD—is a testimony to the power of His love.

Of no one else in history could it be said, "He has done all things well." Napoleon, the great French general, said of Jesus, "I know men and I tell you that Jesus Christ is no mere man. Between Him and every other person in the world there is no possible term of comparison." The genius of Christ's empire was profound, lucid love breaking in to the world since the very beginning of history, and even before time.

At first glance, when we read of Jesus as the Messenger of the LORD appearing in the Old Testament and in New Testament days, we wonder, *How could this possibly be?* However, living in post-Einstein days, we see a glimpse of how this can be in terms of the theory of relativity. Again, Einstein has said, "No one can read the Gospels without feeling the actual presence of Jesus. His personality pulsates every word. No myth is filled with such life."

The very name of *Jesus*, rooted in the Hebrew *"Joshua"* or *"Yeshua,"* means "God saves!" The God who shows up in the Bible has a name in the Old and New Testament that means "God saves!" Salvation unto us has come.

"The first principle of all good theology," Frederick Dale Bruner said, is that "only God can *save.*" When Jesus shows up as the Messenger of God to split the Red Sea, Moses declares, "Stand still and see how the LORD is going to *save* (*Yeshua*) you today!" (Exodus 14:13). Salvation in the Person of Jesus did just that.

It is a shame that the name of Jesus in Exodus 14:13 is glossed over by Bible scholars. As the Messenger of God, six verses later, the One doing the saving, He is identified explicitly. True to form, the Bible scholars go into their glossing-over mode. This happens over and over again by scholars, who, locked into a closed universe, miss the magnificent. In their finite systems, they have no room for the Infinite God who shows up.

Any fair face-value reading of the Scriptures reveals how theology is Christology. The Holy Spirit in miraculous fashion shows how the Bible is given to us for the sake of seeing clearly the God who shows up. The *Kadosh Ruah*, the Holy Spirit, reveals how Jesus calls Abraham out of a world of polytheism into a Kingdom of grace. He reveals how Jesus saves Jacob from himself. He reveals how He calls Moses by the Gospel in the burning bush encounter. He reveals how the Messenger of the LORD provides Sarah with a miracle baby and Samson's parents with a miracle baby, all to foreshadow His miraculous birth. All of this is part of the salvation story. It is designed to ready us for the miracle birth of Jesus.

Bruner, in *The Christbook*, which is his fine commentary on the Gospel of Matthew, reveals how God's ways are not our ways. Certainly the death of the Messiah on the cross bears that out. In the Old Testament it is revealed that cursed is he who dies on a tree (see Deuteronomy 21:23). Yet for us, Jesus, the God who shows up, took that curse upon His sinless shoulders, to free us from the curse of the law (see Galatians 3:13).

This scandal of particularity runs all the way through the Bible. God has particular ways in which He reveals to conceal so that we might become people of faith and love. It is all part of His salvation plan. Without His scandal of particularity, there is no answer to the scandals of hate, greed, lust, alienation, and death.

If there was one word that could summarize the whole Bible, it would be the word *"salvation."* From Genesis to Revelation, the Bible is the story of how God saves us by grace through the perfect work of the God who shows up, namely, His beloved, only begotten Son. Bruner takes note of this:

Jesus is to be the rare person whose name means exactly what it says. "God saves" is not only Jesus' name, it is his perfect definition.... Jesus is God himself who saves us himself. At the same time, the Name *Jesus* (or Joshua) was a common man's name, and Jesus is an entirely human being. How Jesus is both entirely human and entirely divine and how he is both without either 'entirety' cancelling or diluting the other, is the great mystery of Christendom (*The Christbook*, p. 25).

A powerful snapshot of the salvation story, of how the God who shows up transcends time and space, comes from Luke's Gospel. It is the story of the transfiguration of Jesus. It pulls together so much of what we have set forth.

This story is placed by Luke just after Jesus as the Bread of Life fed 5,000 with the five loaves and two fish (see Luke 9:10–16). It comes just after Jesus predicts how He must be rejected by the elders, rulers, priests, and Bible scholars, be killed, and then rise on the third day (see Luke 9:22).

Then Jesus makes another prediction. It is startling. He states how some standing there with Him would never taste death until they saw a dazzling display of God's Kingdom (see Luke 9:27). The transfiguration account describes a burning bush–like glorified appearance of Christ on the eighth day after this prediction. Luke records:

And it came to pass after these words, about eight days, taking along Peter and John and James, Jesus went up to the mountain to pray.

And it came to pass while he was praying the appearance of his face became different and his clothing dazzling white.

*And behold, two men were conversing with him, who were Moses and Elijah, who, having appeared in glory, were speaking about his **exodus**, which he was about to fulfill in Jerusalem* (Luke 9:28–31).

While the disciples were sleeping upon this holy mountain, a celestial summit took place. Remember how Moses encountered Jesus at Mount Horeb in Exodus 3? Where Jesus appeared as the Messenger of the LORD? Remember how Elijah encountered Jesus at Mount Horeb centuries later? Jesus appeared again as the Messenger of the LORD (see 1 Kings 19).

Here all three meet at once. It is a time-warp experience. Just as Jesus made forty-year-old-like delicious wine in one second, Jesus was showing once again His mastery over time and space and age considerations. He is Lord!

Suddenly, Jesus was meeting with these two premier prophets. Jesus Himself had commissioned Moses to go to Egypt to lead in the freeing of God's people from slavery. This occurred around 1500 BC. Then around 900 BC, Jesus came to lift up Elijah. The latter was burnt out from his brutal battles with Queen Jezebel. A bounty was on his head. Wanted: dead or alive, but mostly dead.

Luke records how all three figures were illuminating the glory of their heavenly bodies. Moses and Elijah were there to witness that Jesus was the center of the Old Testament. In a way they were also to return the favor of all the support they had received from Jesus in their ministries on earth. Jesus, in His state of humiliation, no doubt appreciated it. Later, Luke in Acts would, through Peter, declare, *"All the prophets declare that through His name everyone who believes in Him receives forgiveness for his sins"* (Acts 10:43).

Ah, the great Gospel gift—forgiveness of sins. As Luther said, "Wherever there is forgiveness of sins, there is life and salvation." There is also love, joy, peace, patience, kindness, goodness, gentleness, faithfulness, and self-control. These are the Spirit-born, God-who-shows-up-born virtues. This fruit makes a world beautiful as opposed to barbaric.

Back to Luke:

A Mount Horeb reunion was occurring. A back-to-the-future moment was stirring. All of heaven was purring. Billions of heavenly eyes and ears were on Moses, Elijah, and Jesus speaking about the rising Messiah bringing to climax His atonement work.

The weave became even tighter. Luke records how they were talking about Jesus' forthcoming trip to Jerusalem. There, He as Victim and Priest, was to be the Yom Kippur sacrifice for the sins of the cosmos (see John 1:29; 2 Corinthians 5:19–21; Isaiah 53; Genesis 3:15). More than that, if there could be more, they were talking about the greatest *exodus*, which was to come. That is the exact word used in the Greek in Luke 9:31.

Moses had witnessed the dramatic exodus from Egypt, where Jesus split the Red Sea and saved by water the children of Israel (see Exodus 14:19). As the Messenger of God and the One Mediator between God and Man, Jesus "saved" God's people (see Exodus 14:13). What an exodus Moses witnessed. It was the signature salvation event in the Old Testament, designed to point to an even greater exodus to come.

Elijah's exodus was none too shabby, either. A fiery chariot with fiery horses escorted Elijah to a whirlwind that took him to heaven without his seeing death. What a departure from this world, revealing that Jesus as the Messenger of the LORD is LORD over death (see 2 Kings 1:3; 2:11).

Now the God who showed up, born of the Virgin Mary, who showed up to visit Moses repeatedly and to visit Elijah dramatically, brought together all three. He came in grace, not bound by time and space. It is a royal remarkable record that no collection of editors could write and weave with such coherence over 1,500 years. Delightful Divine data!

The exodus that the exodus men were speaking about would become the greatest exodus in history. It would top the Red Sea exodus. It would surpass Elijah's defying-gravity-and-death experience.

On the third day after Jesus' death, the bands and bonds of the grave would be ripped open by the same Messenger of the LORD who provided the power for Exodus 1 and Exodus 2. Jesus the Messiah, *the* Messenger of the LORD, would *bodily* rise from the dead, making an exodus that would breathe into a weary world huge heavenly hope. His resurrection power, the Bible tells us, is *ongoing*. Paul uses a perfect tense in the Greek in 1 Corinthians 15:3–4 to underscore that point.

Jesus died. Past tense. Aorist.

He was buried. Past tense. Aorist.

He rose. Perfect tense. This signifies a past event with future *ongoing* power! He still shows up! But how?

Peter tells us that the ongoing power in holy baptism flows from the bodily resurrection of the Lord Jesus (see 1 Peter 3:21). In every Lord's Supper, it is the power of the risen Lord Jesus Christ at work, not bound by time and space, giving us a heavenly transfusion of grace upon grace through this means of grace (see 1 Corinthians 10:16). This is the true fountain of youth, the medicine of immortality, and the ultimate manna from heaven!

In that latter verse, 1 Corinthians 10:16, Paul uses a grammatical construction in the Greek to underscore *the real presence* of Jesus' body and blood in the Lord's Supper. This New Testament Passover Meal surpasses the Passover Meal of the Old Testament. That glorious meal, also first instituted by the Lord Jesus, was also far more than mere bread and wine (1 Timothy 2:5; Exodus 12:1-13).

Feathering out the **Greek construction** in 1 Corinthians 10:16, the verse carries with it this sense: *Is not the cup of blessing the actual participation of the body of Christ? Of course it is! Is not the bread we break the actual participation of the body of Christ? Of course it is!* This verse testifies to the ongoing *resurrection* power of Christ operative through the Lord's Supper.

Renowned scholar and preacher, now in heaven, Dr. Oswald Hoffman was once asked what is the difference between Christianity and all the other religions of the world. In his rich baritone voice, he boomed, *"The resurrection of the Lord Jesus Christ from the dead!"*

Hoffman, throughout his life, duly noted that the life of Jesus was a story humans simply were unable to make up. As a former Greek professor, he saw patterns and repetitions in the Bible that produced marvelous Messianic meter and meaning. As a worldwide traveler, Hoffman knew that the Bible reads us far better than we read it.

Years ago I wrote a book titled *The Seduction of Extremes*. The central point? Christianity alone as a worldview provides the balanced content for people to recognize the extremes, and, by the grace of the God who shows up, avoid them! The reason today that we see the wild pendulum swings of people in the Western world is that they reside in a world not anchored in God's grace in Christ.

In *The Seduction of Extremes*, I also noted that Christianity is the only religion that gives a damn, because the God who showed up was willing to be damned for us. In no other religion does its deity enter into our plight, problems, and peril. The gods of other religions are far, far removed from offering a helping hand to the misery of the masses. Jesus is so, so very different. For us and for all, Jesus undergoes abject abysmal humiliation to lead us to our glorification by the road of the cross and the open tomb.

For the Christian, the message of the Bible is that we are more than conquerors through Christ who loved us (see Romans 8:37). That is the same message of the book of Daniel as well as the book of Revelation. Please note that there is no "*s*" at the end of Revelation. I had a professor in seminary who told the students in our class that he would flunk anyone who mispronounced the book as "Revelations," for there are no new revelations beyond the Bible. No one dared tested his resolve.

THE GOD WHO SHOWED UP

I bring up the books of Revelation and Daniel because both books assure us that God is working everything together in history for the good of Christ's Bride, the Church (see Ephesians 1:22).

The sovereignty of the Triune God for the sake of the Gospel needs to be part of our regular fare, for we live in a time when the world is rapidly unraveling. By all signs, it appears we are living in the last days of the end times. The overall counsel of Luther still stands: *We should live as though Christ died yesterday, rose today, and is coming tomorrow.* Since the book of Revelation is written for every age, prophetic reserve tempers us even as the explosion of knowledge emboldens us (see Revelation 1:3; Daniel 12:4). Those who are wise will lead people to righteousness, to the God who shows up, to Jesus Christ (see Daniel 12:3).

In Matthew 25:31–46, Jesus tells us what to expect when He reappears in glory. Even now He is present with us as God and man filling the whole universe (see Colossians 1:15–20; 2:9). His humanity cannot be torn from His divinity. He is Lord.

When He does reappear in glory, history as we know it will grind to a sudden halt. History will not end by global warming nor by human chicanery. The whole intoxicated notion that humans can save the world when we cannot even *create* a mosquito is high hubris. The world will end by fiat of the Lord Jesus. Just as Jesus willed to die at the exact moment on Good Friday that the Passover Lamb was slain, so will Jesus end history at the exact moment in time of His glorious appearing . He is Lord.

In Matthew's account of a preview of coming attractions, Jesus declares He will return with all His holy angels with Him (Matthew 25:31-46). John, in Revelation 1:7, reveals that every eye will see Him. Paul writes in 1 Corinthians 15:52 that every ear will hear Him. From our first parents, Adam and Eve, to the last child ever conceived—all will be present. He is Lord.

People will be divided along one of two lines: sheep or goats, believers or unbelievers, followers of the Good Shepherd or followers of the old evil foe. Jesus makes it clear that salvation is a gift. He uses Gospel words like "blessed," "inherit," and "prepared for you before the foundation of the world." Most commentators shoot right by this triad of Gospel revelations. The result? They confuse fruits with roots. Human-works righteousness overshadows Christ's gift of righteousness. They miss how the sheep are saved by grace and the goats choose to be left to their own law resources.

For the sheep, the followers of the Good Shepherd, grazing on grace is the only place to be on Judgment Day. While Jesus' lambs are saved by grace alone through faith in Christ, nevertheless, Jesus will reward them for the good works they do out of love for Him. Cool cosmic grace. He rewards us for the good works He moves us to do. Double grace!

Big little thing—BLT! Jesus does not bring up a single solitary sin of the believers. He judges the sheep in mercy. He saves us by grace. "There is therefore now no condemnation to those in Christ Jesus" (Romans 8:1).

What about the goats—those who prefer living by the law? The news is grim. You live by the law, you will die by the law. You reject the Gospel, you will have the accuser, the devil, as your defense attorney. Imagine that! Your defense attorney will do everything he can to find you guilty and deserving of eternal hell.

The sheep have Jesus Christ as their Judge and Defense Attorney (1 John 2:1-2; 2 Corinthians 5:10). He has totally paid the bill for our sin. He has perfectly fulfilled the law for us. He gives us His robe of righteousness through baptism. In baptism, Jesus washes away all our sin and makes us descendants of Abraham (see Galatians 3:26–29).

So many people in our Twitter world try reading the Bible and then encounter a massive amount of history that can easily overwhelm them. Added to this, much of the contemporary commentary by experts misses the continuous coherent Christological content of the Bible. My hope is that *The God Who Showed Up* becomes a helpful handle for all who want an Emmaus road experience (see Luke 24:13–35). Keep your eyes on Jesus.

"Anyone who believes in Him will not be disappointed" (Isaiah 28:16; Romans 10:11).

All the best, as far as the east is to the west...in the name of Him who is the Hope, Head, and Hinge of history, Jesus Christ!

—Pastor Peter Kurowski

Messiah-Centered Summary of the Bible

God, in love, in Christ, plans our salvation. It is a Trinitarian work.

Out of nothing, Jesus creates the universe in concert with the Father and the Spirit.

From Adam's side, Jesus forms a beautiful bride.

Jesus gives Adam and Eve a love-and-rescue promise after the Fall.

Jesus saves Noah by water and wood and the Word.

Jesus calls Abraham by the Gospel.

Jesus as Divine Physician promises Abraham and Sarah a miracle baby.

Jesus destroys Sodom and Gomorrah to preserve the Remnant from a town of sexual predators.

Jesus as the Messenger of the LORD saves Isaac at Mount Moriah, which will become Jerusalem.

Jesus wrestles with Jacob and gives him the name of "Israel" at dawn.

Jesus preserves the Remnant of seventy via His grace and mercy granted to Joseph.

Jesus appears to Moses via a burning bush.

Jesus splits the Red Sea, saving by water Israel of old at dawn.

Jesus as the Rock preserves Israel for forty years.

Jesus as the Messenger of the LORD raises judges to rescue a wayward Israel.

Jesus grants Israel permission to have kings.

Jesus protects the Remnant and takes out 185,000 Assyrian soldiers at dawn.

Jesus reenergizes, body, soul, and spirit, a burnt-out prophet, Elijah.

Jesus gives Isaiah the ability to predict the Virgin Birth.

Jesus gives Isaiah the ability to see the events of Good Friday and Easter.

Jesus saves the three men in the fiery furnace.

Jesus, the Lion of Judah, saves Daniel from the lion's den at dawn.

Jesus comes to Zechariah repeatedly in visions.

Jesus' Spirit causes Mary to become the mother of God.

Jesus perfectly fulfills the Law of God at all times...going to Egypt, living in Nazareth, and more.

Jesus, at age twelve, dazzles Israel's greatest teachers.

Jesus is baptized for us, taking on our sin to give us His righteousness.

Jesus walks on water, raises the dead, and does everything that the Messiah is predicted to do.

Jesus preaches the greatest sermon on love ever—the Sermon on the Mount.

Jesus preaches the greatest funeral sermon ever preached when He raises Lazarus from the dead.

Jesus institutes the Lord's Supper, the medicine of immortality.

Jesus suffers hell upon the cross on a skull-shaped hill.

Jesus suffers for all sinners, once for all, upon Golgotha.

Jesus' body is made alive and He preaches a victory sermon in the devil's own backyard.

Holy angels tell the good news of Jesus' bodily resurrection at dawn.

Jesus appears as the risen Savior to His disciples and to others repeatedly.

Jesus promises to be with His disciples through Word and Sacrament.

Jesus as the Temple ascends to fill all things and to dwell within His followers.

Jesus sends the Holy Spirit to fulfill what the prophet Joel promised.

Jesus sends the Spirit, providing Pentecost and four major events in Acts to show that the Gospel is for all.

The Spirit of Jesus breaks down walls, takes down slavery, and advances the sanctity of life.

Jesus comes to us in Holy Baptism, Holy Communion, Holy Absolution, and the Holy Gospel.

Jesus takes His followers to Paradise immediately upon their death.

Jesus binds the work of the devil substantially as the Gospel goes to all people.

The devil is set free for a little while, attacking Christ's Bride, the Church.

Jesus sends fire from heaven to consume the devil and his minions.

Jesus returns to judge all—and every eye will see Him.

Believers in Christ are judged, but not condemned, judged in mercy instead.

Unbelievers who try to live by the law will die by the law, ending up in the lake of fire.

The world is destroyed and purified by fire simultaneously.

The new heaven and the new earth comes forth! Animals will also be there!

Believers are given new, glorified bodies—forever young. Huge upgrades!

Believers behold God face-to-face, full restoration to the new Eden is regained forever!

Prayed on the Dais Where State of the Union Address Is Given

*L*ord God, enlighten us to see that unless You build the house, in vain the artisans toil; and unless You stand sentry upon a nation, in vain do our guardians watch. Open our eyes to see Your awesome fingerprints in creation, Your amazing footprints in the realm of redemption, and Your architectural imprints upon the documents which helped to give birth to this Republic. May these revelations move citizens everywhere to walk humbly, do justice, and show compassion. Inspire a desire in Americans everywhere to absorb the Biblical book of Ecclesiastes so that as a nation we do not repeat the melancholy moments of history. We ask this in the name of the Wisdom of the ages, the Savior of sinners, Jesus Christ. Amen. Amen.

—Prayer delivered on the House floor
by Dr. Peter M. Kurowski, June 8, 1999

This prayer reflects how "the God who showed up" impacted the birth of our Republic via the practice of Christian chaplains from the beginning.

CPSIA information can be obtained
at www.ICGtesting.com
Printed in the USA
FFOW05n1900250816

9 781457 548024